Bach against Modernity

Bach against Modernity

MICHAEL MARISSEN

OXFORD
UNIVERSITY PRESS

Oxford University Press is a department of the University of Oxford. It furthers
the University's objective of excellence in research, scholarship, and education
by publishing worldwide. Oxford is a registered trade mark of Oxford University
Press in the UK and certain other countries.

Published in the United States of America by Oxford University Press
198 Madison Avenue, New York, NY 10016, United States of America.

© Oxford University Press 2023

All rights reserved. No part of this publication may be reproduced, stored in
a retrieval system, or transmitted, in any form or by any means, without the
prior permission in writing of Oxford University Press, or as expressly permitted
by law, by license, or under terms agreed with the appropriate reproduction
rights organization. Inquiries concerning reproduction outside the scope of the
above should be sent to the Rights Department, Oxford University Press, at the
address above.

You must not circulate this work in any other form
and you must impose this same condition on any acquirer.

CIP data is on file at the Library of Congress
ISBN 978-0-19-766949-5

DOI: 10.1093/oso/9780197669495.001.0001

Printed by Sheridan Books, Inc., United States of America

For Lauren

Contents

Preface	ix
Credits	xv

PART I. CONSTRAINTS OF HISTORY ON INTERPRETATION

1. Bach against Modernity	3
2. Bach's Handwritten Entries in His Bible	31

PART II. BRIEF COMMENTARIES

3. Fractal Gavottes and the Ephemeral World in Bach's Cantata 64	53
4. Time and Eternities in Bach's Cantata 23	58
5. Bach's *Christmas Oratorio* and a Blessed End	64
6. Bach and Art and Mammon	68

PART III. TEXTS

7. Historically Informed Renderings of the Librettos from Bach's Cantatas (with coauthor Daniel R. Melamed)	73

PART IV. JEWS AND JUDAISM

8. On the Jews and Their So-Called Lies in the Fourth Gospel and Bach's *St. John Passion*	137

viii CONTENTS

9. Bach and Sons in the Jewish Salon Culture of
   Nineteenth-Century Berlin   146

PART V. THEOLOGICAL CHARACTER OF
SECULAR INSTRUMENTAL MUSIC

10. Bach's Sacred *Brandenburg Concertos*   157

11. The Serious Nature of the Quodlibet in Bach's
    Goldberg Variations   163

Works Cited   173
Index of Bach's Works   181
Index of Names and Subjects   183

Preface

This book is a follow-up to a recent volume called *Bach & God*. Both are collections of essays first published mostly in academic journals and then brought together for a broader audience. I had entertained the idea of naming the new volume *Bach & God 2*, but this seemed a bit unserious. *More Bach & God* suggested itself as a fitting title—some may have hoped for *More Bach, Less God*—but then I realized that it would be most effective to go with the name of the compilation's lead essay and call the book *Bach against Modernity*.

All eleven essays in this volume delve into or touch on the subject of Bach and modernity. Each can, however, be read as a standalone. None of them assumes expert background knowledge of music, religion, or history.

The two chapters of part I concern broad problems of inattentiveness to historical considerations in academic and popular writing about Bach's relation to the present.

Chapter 1 has its origins in an invitation I received to give the keynote address in a scholarly symposium at the University of Massachusetts–Amherst entitled "Bach in the Age of Modernism, Postmodernism, and Globalization." The idea, apparently, although it was not specified, was that I would speak on Bach as a modern figure. I had great qualms about that, however, as I had always thought of Bach as a pre-Enlightenment (i.e., premodern) figure, and so I was inclined to turn down the request. But my spouse soon hazarded the inspired suggestion that I ought to ask if it would be acceptable for me to deliver a lecture entitled "Bach *against* Modernity." The organizers at first seemed taken aback by this

X PREFACE

proposition, but they agreed that such a topic was likely to generate a lot of discussion. As an expanded version of the lecture, chapter 1 argues that Bach reflected and forcefully promoted a premodern world- and life view, both in his documented personal life and in his public music.

Chapter 2 has its origins in a brief essay for the *New York Times* about the premodern theological and philosophical content of Bach's various hand-penned annotations in his personal Bible, occasioned by the long-awaited publication, in the Netherlands, of a luxurious color facsimile of those three massive volumes. The essay generated a good bit of interest, and this prompted me to expand the material into a longer article for the scholarly journal *Lutheran Quarterly*. Chapter 2, then, argues that on account of their lack of proper familiarity with the Lutheran historical background and foreground of Bach's life and works, leading writers have seriously misread both Bach's music and his Bible annotations as "modern." They have interpreted Bach's annotations as supporting their images of the composer as a quasi-Freudian, identity-crisis-ridden genius; or as a quasi-scientific, learned empiricist scholar; or as a quasi-pantheistic, broadly ecumenical aesthete; or as a Great Artist finding special creative stimuli to compose individual works. With wider and deeper knowledge of relevant historical materials, however, these views rather look like contextually improbable anachronisms—impositions of a modern mindset on an early-eighteenth-century figure.

The four chapters of part II concern brief but close critical rehearing of key individual works of Bach's.

Chapter 3 has its origins in a YouTube talk, for the American Bach Society's series *Tiny Bach Concerts*, that provided interpretive background for a video performance of the soprano aria from Bach's Cantata 64 by Maria Keohane, soprano, and Fredrik From, violin, with Concerto Copenhagen, directed by Lars Ulrik Mortensen. This chapter argues that Bach's strange, systematic disintegration of a dance form in this aria was designed to highlight several main themes in a premodern Lutheran viewpoint that was continually pitted against what conservative Lutherans like him took to be the undue and indeed dangerous optimism of Enlightenment thinking: his aria setting proclaims that the present world is fundamentally not good, that humanism and its attainments ultimately add up to nothing (people cannot fundamentally or reliably make the world better), and that only eternity, not problematic time, is cast-iron (the temporal world, with its ephemeral delights, will fade away).

Chapter 4 has its origins in "Bach and Jesus," an informal virtual roundtable with my colleagues Robin Leaver and Noelle Heber for a new video journal from BachNetwork.org called *Discussing Bach*. This chapter argues that the "existential I" of Bach's Cantata 23 is not a modern individual who achieves ultimate fulfillment through one's own effort, merit, and accomplishment but a member of an eternal community on whom personal salvation "befalls," through the unmerited gift of divine grace. And so Cantata 23, which was one of Bach's Leipzig audition pieces, can be heard not simply as an aesthetic manifesto of a modern Great Artist (as is sometimes suggested) but as a sort of theological-musical manifesto: *this* is what music can do, music can project depths of biblical and theological meaning and experience in ways that words alone cannot.

Chapter 5 has its origins in an informal preconcert talk entitled "Bach's *Christmas Oratorio* and the Final Advent of God's Messiah," delivered in conjunction with a performance of Bach's *Christmas Oratorio* by the Bach Collegium of Japan, directed by Masaaki Suzuki, at Lincoln Center for the Performing Arts in New York City. This chapter argues that Bach, in his fiftieth year and pondering his death, set the end of the *Christmas Oratorio* in a particular way in light of his individual (and communal) hope for what his Lutheranism called "a blessed end" (namely, to depart from this life into the glory of a blessed afterlife in heaven). That is to say, Bach did *not* long for posthumous fame and glory as a modern, autonomous Great Artist.

xii PREFACE

Chapter 6 has its origins as the foreword to a marvelous book by Noelle Heber about Bach and material and spiritual riches. This chapter argues that in Bach's world, the arts appear to have been valued more for spiritual comfort and enjoyment than for the modern, centrally driving ideals of entertainment, amusement, and "pure" aesthetic contemplation.

The one chapter of part III concerns detailed problems in modern comprehension and rendering of the partly archaic German texts that Bach set to music.

Chapter 7 has its origins in a long-term project, now well under way, by Daniel Melamed and me to prepare annotated translations of all the librettos from Bach's church cantatas, secular cantatas, and motets. In this jointly written chapter, he and I discuss the various kinds of technical issues premodern German vocabulary, historical Lutheran theology, interpretively significant biblical allusion, editorial problems of establishing proper source texts—that do or should plague historically informed translators of such material.

The two chapters of part IV concern Bach's music and premodern versus enlightened attitudes toward Jews and Judaism.

Chapter 8 has its origins in an overview essay I was asked to write for the booklet accompanying a major label's new recording of Bach's *St. John Passion*. The essay, alas, got spiked, as it focused heavily on questions of anti-Judaism, a subject that, according to the recording's producers, today's general readers and listeners are not ready for. So I decided to expand the materials a bit and successfully pitched them to the magazine *Lutheran Forum*. This chapter suggests that Bach arguably went far beyond the call of duty in musically depicting Jewish opposition to Jesus in a series of biblical choruses for the *St. John Passion* that center on what Luther, in his *On the Jews and Their Lies* of 1543 (a screed that Bach himself owned), had deemed the most fundamental of Jewish lies. The scholarly notion that there appears to have been in Bach's Leipzig a maturing spirit of openness and fairness toward Jews, such that by the 1730s, the times had indeed changed and that thus it would have been unlikely to encounter anti-Jewish reflection within the sermons and the choral music delivered in the city's churches, is shown by recent repertorial discoveries to have been radically oversanguine.

Chapter 9 has its origins in an invitation from the editor, in Jerusalem, of a Jewish women's studies journal to write a wide-ranging review of a commercial recording of mid- and late-eighteenth-century chamber music performed by Rebecca Cypess and the Raritan Players called *In Sara Levy's Salon*. This chapter relates how at Sara Levy's nineteenth-century Berlin salons, men and women, Jews and Christians, aristocrats and bourgeois, all gathered to drink tea and eat finger food; engage in convivial conversation about literature, art, philosophy, and politics; and hear performances of instrumental music composed by J. S. Bach and his sons. The chapter, further, suggests that Levy's programs consisted mostly of serious but somewhat "abstract" types of music, repertory that as a rule was without emphatic religious, social-class, or gendered associations, and that such intellectually satisfying and emotionally sanguine art as this must have seemed perfectly fitting and appealing in the context of the optimistic Enlightenment ideals of the illustrious Jews and Christians known to have attended her events.

The two chapters of part V concern the theological character of Bach's secular instrumental music.

Chapter 10 is a brief essay, originally printed in the *New York Times*, on the persistent myth that Bach's music is marked by a fundamental conflict between the sacred and the secular. This chapter suggests that listeners and scholars who speak in this way about Bach understand the terms "sacred" and "secular" in a modern, anachronistic way, namely, to mean "having to do with God" versus "not having to do with God." The chapter, further, argues that Bach's *Brandenburg Concertos*, typically now regarded as quintessentially "pure" instrumental music, can with greater historical awareness be thought of as a wordless "sacred" repertory that does project theological and social meanings.

xiv PREFACE

Finally, chapter 11 has its origins in an article for the magazine *CrossAccent: Journal of the Association of Lutheran Church Musicians* regarding new discoveries about the ostensible merry old German folk-song sources for the Quodlibet from Bach's *Goldberg Variations*. This chapter argues that Bach, by having in truth combined a *hymn* and a folk song, wrote the work not as jokesome entertainment or as self-expression but as an act of premodern Lutheran tribute to the heavenly and earthly realms of God.

*

For encouragement and expert advice, I would like to especially thank my great professional colleagues and great personal friends Anthony Godzieba, Daniel Melamed, and Bettina Varwig.

I also benefited tremendously from the insightful comments of two anonymous reviewers for Oxford University Press.

My thanks also to Norm Hirschy (Senior Editor, Music Books, Oxford University Press) for his support. Likewise to Nick Ashman (Editorial Assistant, OUP), Rachel Ruisard (Project Editor, OUP), Leslie Johnson (Senior Production Editor, OUP), and Jubilee James (Project Manager, Newgen Knowledge Works).

Profound thanks, too, to Wendy Keebler for expert copyediting and Rachel Perkins for the marvelous cover design.

Once again, above all, I thank Lauren Belfer. Once again, she knows the reasons why.

Credits

The previously published essays in this volume, lightly edited or updated or both, are reprinted here with permission.

A version of chapter 1 originally appeared as "Bach against Modernity," in *Rethinking Bach*, edited by Bettina Varwig (New York: Oxford University Press, 2021), 315–335.

A version of chapter 2 originally appeared as "The Biographical Significance of Bach's Handwritten Entries in His Calov Bible," *Lutheran Quarterly* 34 (2020): 373–389; a much shorter version had appeared as "Johann Sebastian Bach Was More Religious Than You Might Think," *New York Times*, Sunday Arts & Leisure section, April 1, 2018.

A version of chapter 3 originally appeared as American Bach Society, *Tiny Bach Concerts*, Episode 8 (2021), remarks by Michael Marissen; performance by Maria Keohane, soprano; Fredrik From, violin; with Concerto Copenhagen, directed by Lars Ulrik Mortensen. https://www.youtube.com/watch?v=i_Mgvr4-SN0.

A version of chapter 4 originally appeared as "Jesus in Time and Eternity," in Robin A. Leaver, Noelle M. Heber, and Michael Marissen, "Bach and Jesus," *Discussing Bach* 2 (2021): 2–17. https://bachnetwork.org/discussing-bach/db2/.

Chapter 5 was excerpted and adapted from a preconcert lecture at the performance of Bach's *Christmas Oratorio* by the Bach Collegium of Japan, director Masaaki Suzuki, December 6, 2017, *Great Performers Series*, Lincoln Center, New York.

A version of chapter 6 originally appeared as "Foreword," in Noelle M. Heber, *J. S. Bach's Material and Spiritual Treasures: A Theological Perspective* (Woodbridge, UK: Boydell Press, 2021), xiii–xiv.

All the materials in chapter 7, appearing here by permission of the authors, are excerpted from a long-term project, in preparation, by Daniel R. Melamed and Michael Marissen, *Texts and Historically Informed Translations for the Music of Johann Sebastian Bach.* http://bachcantatatexts.org.

A version of chapter 8 originally appeared as "On the Jews and Their So-Called Lies in the Fourth Gospel and Bach's *St. John Passion*," *Lutheran Forum* 54, no. 4 (2020): 35–38.

A version of chapter 9 originally appeared as "Rebecca Cypess & the Raritan Players, *In Sara Levy's Salon* (compact disc, Acis Productions, 2017)," *Nashim: A Journal of Jewish Women's Studies & Gender Issues* 34 (2019): 196–201.

The main text of chapter 10 originally appeared, verbatim, in "There's More Religion Than You Think in Bach's 'Brandenburgs,'" *New York Times*, Sunday Arts & Leisure section, December 23, 2018.

A version of chapter 11 originally appeared as "The Serious Nature of the Quodlibet in Bach's *Goldberg Variations*," *CrossAccent: Journal of the Association of Lutheran Church Musicians* 29, no. 3 (2021): 40–45.

PART I
CONSTRAINTS OF HISTORY ON INTERPRETATION

1
Bach against Modernity

A number of philosophically adroit studies arguing for or against the idea that Johann Sebastian Bach and his music project a modern worldview have been published recently by Karol Berger, John Butt, Bettina Varwig, Jeremy Begbie, and Harry White.[1] These studies center largely on apparent conceptions of time in modern and premodern thought.

I see great value in approaching the subject of Bach and modernity differently, though, and so I do not think the present discussion ought to be framed specifically by the arguments of my learned predecessors. If I might be forgiven for speaking rather bluntly, I think there is something to be said for devoting less attention to the abstract theories of Theodor W. Adorno, Mikhail Bakhtin, Walter Benjamin, Hans-Georg Gadamer, Michel Foucault, or Fredric Jameson (as much as I, too, believe that one can benefit from perusing these authors) and more attention to the substantive

---

[1] Karol Berger, *Bach's Cycle, Mozart's Arrow: An Essay on the Origins of Musical Modernity* (Berkeley: University of California Press, 2007); John Butt, *Bach's Dialogue with Modernity: Perspectives on the Passions* (Cambridge: Cambridge University Press, 2010); Bettina Varwig, "Metaphors of Time and Modernity in Bach," *Journal of Musicology* 29 (2012): 154–190; Jeremy Begbie, "Disquieting Conversations: Bach, Modernity, and God," in Jeremy Begbie, *Music, Modernity, and God* (New York: Oxford University Press, 2013), 41–72; Harry White, "Evangelists of the Postmodern: Reconfigurations of Bach since 1985," *Understanding Bach* 12 (2017): 85–107; and Harry White, "The Steward of Unmeaning Art: Bach and the Musical Subject," in Harry White, *The Musical Discourse of Servitude: Authority, Autonomy, and the Work-Concept in Fux, Bach, and Handel* (New York: Oxford University Press, 2020), 110–148. Note that Begbie tactfully draws attention to Butt's and Berger's in some cases serious misunderstandings of central aspects of Christianity in general and Reformation theology in particular. On Bach as premodern, see also Michael Marissen, "The Biographical Significance of Bach's Handwritten Entries in His Calov Bible," *Lutheran Quarterly* 34 (2020): 373–389 (reprinted as chapter 2 in the present volume).

Bach against Modernity. Michael Marissen, Oxford University Press. © Oxford University Press 2023.
DOI: 10.1093/oso/9780197669495.003.0001

4 CONSTRAINTS OF HISTORY ON INTERPRETATION

Bach repertory and the primary sources that are directly associated with Bach.

Even if one does want to consider philosophical material on apparent attitudes toward time in Bach as truly central to our topic, rather than speculating about which writings of which leading Enlightenment thinkers Bach may (doubtfully?) resonate with, why not at least start, as no one has yet done, by investigating the Lutheran theologian Martin Geier's nearly two-thousand-page book on time and eternity, which was reprinted several times in the eighteenth century and is known to have been in Bach's personal library?[2] (Geier, incidentally, was the superintendent of the Leipzig churches from 1661 to 1665, and to this day, you can see a stern portrait of him clutching a Bible in his left hand gracing the altar area of the Thomaskirche in Leipzig.)

When it comes to sorting out properly which precise biblical or scientific notions of linear time (versus cyclical time) truly shed light on Bach, it appears we do not have much that is of use to go on.[3] Geier's tomes only reinforce this estimation: linear notions of passing time, often held now to be "modern," also run deeply through premodern, biblically based thought.

This chapter will, instead, touch briefly on a whole series of more probative, workable, and down-to-earth topics, and they will turn out strongly to place Bach against modernity.

All three of these words—"Bach," "against," and "modernity"—carry multiple meanings, but I do not wish to get bogged down in formulating bulletproof definitions for them.

---

[2] Martin Geier, *Zeit und Ewigkeit* (Leipzig, 1670; reprints, e.g., in 1702 and 1738). Augustinian and other theories of time are discussed in I:565–587; see also I:10–30. For details on the theological books known to have been in Bach's library, see Robin A. Leaver, *Bachs theologische Bibliothek* (Neuhausen-Stuttgart: Hänssler-Verlag, 1985). Several of these books and other affinitive volumes are examined, with great insight and with close attention to their direct evidentiary relevance for conceptions of time in Bach's milieu, in Varwig, "Metaphors of Time and Modernity."

[3] As explained in Begbie, "Disquieting Conversations," 53–69.

Suffice it to say, I hope, that by "Bach," I will mean mostly "Bach's music" and only sometimes "Bach the human being."

By "against," I will mean mostly "opposed in tendency to" and sometimes "compared with."

As for "modernity," this is an extremely thorny concept, especially in connection with theology or religion, but for our purposes, I will follow the philosopher Louis Dupré's closely argued crystallization,[4] understanding the "modern" in "modernity" to mean:

- exalting reason above revelation—whatever the flaws of reason—as arbiter of truth
- exalting human autonomy and achievement
- exalting religious tolerance
- exalting cosmopolitanism
- exalting social and political progressiveness

You may wish immediately to object that if Bach is indeed *against* modernity in these various ways, how on earth has he come to be so deeply valued in modern times by such wide audiences? This is a good question but one that goes beyond the scope of the present chapter and deserves special study,[5] and so all I will say here is that my experiences, developed over several decades of general-audience and academic lecturing in hundreds of universities, colleges, churches, and synagogues, have led me to conclude that a great many music lovers do not, strictly speaking, value Bach for the things he may, strictly speaking, be about.

Now, it is true that some people want only to be entertained. But I am with the narrator of Richard Russo's marvelous academic

---

[4] Louis Dupré, *Passage to Modernity* (New Haven, CT: Yale University Press, 1993). It is ultimately impossible to come up with one single transhistorically valid, "essential" definition of modernity.

[5] Butt (*Bach's Dialogue with Modernity*) does explore this question but through philosophical rumination, not through the weighing of explicitly stated points of view among broadly diverse audiences.

6 CONSTRAINTS OF HISTORY ON INTERPRETATION

novel *Straight Man*, when he says (my emphasis), "It's been my experience that most people don't want to be entertained. They want to be *comforted*."[6]

What I hear time and again from Bach lovers is that they derive great hope, comfort, and joy from his music. Many Christians have told me that they find profound sustenance in the Christianity of Bach's music, while many nonbelievers in Jesus have told me that they are moved to powerful feelings of hope, comfort, and joy— that is, not merely to what could be called emotions of *aesthetic* exaltation—by the powerfully hopeful, comforting, and joyous sheer sound of the Bach repertory; and they go on to say that they do not feel compelled to connect their powerful feelings to any specific verbal content, Christian or otherwise.

These nonbelievers in Jesus do not deny that Bach's music may be or is really, at base, about Christianity. They simply bracket this aspect of Bach and take from him what they can profitably "use." One has to admire their honesty.

Bach lovers who value only appreciative disinterested aesthetic attention to works of the arts, by contrast, especially scholars,[7] often insist—desperately, it seems to me—that Bach's music is so staggeringly great that his compositions have to be really, at base, about the modern so-called virtues of disinterested "pure" (!) aesthetic attention.[8]

Many Bach lovers, I have also discovered, think of his music as "modern" on account of what are found or sensed to be its "mathematical" or "scientific" qualities, these categories often uncritically understood as essentially secularist and therefore modern. There is no question that Bach's music is *orderly* in the extreme. But Bach

---

[6] Richard Russo, *Straight Man* (New York: Random House, 1997), xi.

[7] See, e.g., David Schulenberg, "'Musical Allegory' Reconsidered: Representation and Imagination in the Baroque," *Journal of Musicology* 13 (1995): 203–239, esp. 238: Bach's music "aims to please, not to instruct or inspire."

[8] That is, as opposed to apparently "impure"/"unclean" emotional or religious attention that can complement or supplement aesthetic attention and pleasure.

may well have simply labored out of the belief that orderliness was next to godliness. "For God is a God of order," he would have read at the commentary on 1 Chronicles 25:1 in his (personally annotated) Calov Bible.[9]

Significance of "J.J." and "S.D.G."?

It is possible that a particular notational practice of Bach's (namely, writing the initials "J.J." or "S.D.G." in certain scores) gives some useful indication of what he considered to be the ultimate general orientation of his musical activities. This notational practice has been widely mentioned and widely interpreted but without, as we will see, having been properly documented or assayed.

A claim for ubiquitous "S.D.G." markings has been made about Bach's cantatas in the promotional materials for the not-for-profit recording label created in 2005 by John Eliot Gardiner with the Monteverdi Choir and the English Baroque Soloists. They state:

> SDG are the initials that J. S. Bach appended at the end of each of his Cantata scores. It stands for Soli Deo Gloria, to the Glory of God alone, and signified his deep devotion and his desire to serve God through his music.
>
> These same initials identify our label, which was initially dedicated to the recordings made during the Bach Cantata Pilgrimage. In total SDG released 27 albums, each corresponding to one of the Bach Cantata Pilgrimage's concerts and including the cantatas Bach wrote for a specific liturgical feast.[10]

---

[9] Abraham Calov, *Die heilige Bibel nach S. Herrn D. Martini Lutheri Deutscher Dolmetschung und Erklärung*, VI parts (Wittenberg, 1681–1682), I:1049: "Denn GOTT ist ein GOTT der Ordnung." See Michael Marissen, *The Social and Religious Designs of J. S. Bach's Brandenburg Concertos* (Princeton, NJ: Princeton University Press, 1995), 113. Bach's own copy of Calov is now kept at the Concordia Seminary Library in St. Louis, Missouri. See also the extensive discussion of Bach's biblical annotations in Marissen, "The Biographical Significance" (reprinted as chapter 2 in the present volume).

[10] https://monteverdi.co.uk/shop/cantata-series.

8 CONSTRAINTS OF HISTORY ON INTERPRETATION

Gardiner's people are referring to Bach's cantatas for the Lutheran liturgy. About 70 percent of Bach's extant church cantatas survive in autograph scores, and although there are a few autograph scores that I have not yet seen, I can report with confidence that about 40 percent of Bach's church cantata scores do not read "S.D.G." at the end.

A more subtle and nuanced claim about these notations was put forward by the great scholar John Butt in his widely read and widely cited essay on Bach's conception of music.[11] Butt is someone who has studied the original Bach scores and performing parts closely,[12] and thus, one should be disposed to imagine that he speaks with full and reliable authority on our subject. His essay states:

> Bach's own comments (and those from his closest circle) concerning the nature and function of music are few and far between. If we turn first to the ultimate purposes of music, the handful of dedications on title pages from Bach's oeuvre present a rather mixed picture. While the title page to the *Orgelbüchlein* presents the "Praise of God" as the foremost aim, none of the others makes this explicit. The standard initials "J.J." ("Jesu juva"—"Jesus help!") and "S.D.G." ("Soli deo gloria"—"To God alone be glory!") are found at the beginning and end of church compositions, and of some, but by no means all, of the secular pieces.[13]

What ought immediately to give pause in this statement is its use of the phrase "by no means." To say "*some* [are found]" might be straightforwardly factual. To say "some, *but not all*" might be to hover between the factual and the interpretive. But to say "some,

---

[11] John Butt, "Bach's Metaphysics of Music," in *The Cambridge Companion to Bach*, ed. John Butt (Cambridge: Cambridge University Press, 1997), 46–59.

[12] See esp. John Butt, *Bach Interpretation: Articulation Markings in the Primary Sources of J. S. Bach* (Cambridge: Cambridge University Press, 1990).

[13] Butt, "Bach's Metaphysics," 52.

but *by no means* all" is a strong expression of negation and is, as such, emphatically interpretive.

Butt's essay does not indicate precisely how widespread the markings are in Bach's compositions, but from what it does say, readers will reasonably come away with the impression that the practice must have been fully in character for Bach's liturgical compositions and somewhat out of character for his secular compositions. And the situation with the secular compositions, Butt's essay appears further to imply, would be the one that truly "counts" in exploring Bach's conception of music in general.

I think it is fair to say that many who claim a high incidence for Bach's "J.J." and "S.D.G." markings do so in a devotionalist belief-based effort to support a notion of Bach as an essentially religious figure[14] and that many who claim, or hint at, a low incidence for Bach's markings in his non-liturgical scores do so in a secularist belief-based effort to support a notion of Bach as an essentially autonomous and aesthetic—that is to say, as an essentially "modern"—figure.

It turns out to be highly instructive to study precisely which of the many Bach autograph scores do contain the inscriptions and which scores do not. From this, one readily sees that the markings are in truth both far from ubiquitous and far from rare.

Where will that bring or leave us?

I would propose looking into whether the rates of Bach's markings fall into significant patterns.

Striking patterns do emerge when you arrange all of Bach's surviving original scores together—liturgical and secular—into chronological groupings.

Consider first Bach's pre-Leipzig tenure. Of these approximately thirty-five surviving autograph scores, only one score is inscribed

---

[14] See, e.g., Rick Marschall, *Christian Encounters: Johann Sebastian Bach* (Nashville: Thomas Nelson, 2011), which claims that Bach began all of his compositions with "J.J." and concluded all of them with "S.D.G."

10 CONSTRAINTS OF HISTORY ON INTERPRETATION

"J.J.," and only two scores are inscribed with one or another form of the "S.D.G." marking; no scores contain both markings. This tally shows that in the earlier part of his career, Bach was aware of the notational practices but almost never saw fit to employ them.

Things changed dramatically with his move to Leipzig.

During the time of his first cantata cycle, most of Bach's scores (about 81 percent) contain "J.J." markings, a few (about 12 percent) contain "S.D.G." markings, and even fewer (about 8 percent) contain both markings.

In his second cycle (the most intensive period of composition in Bach's life), virtually all scores (about 98 percent) contain "J.J." markings, many (about 50 percent) contain "S.D.G." markings, and many (about 48 percent) contain both.

In his third cycle, most scores (about 90 percent) contain "J.J." markings, a majority (about 65 percent) contain "S.D.G." markings, and a majority (about 63 percent) contain both.

Finally, during his later years in Leipzig, a majority of scores (about 61 percent) contain "J.J." markings, many (about 40 percent) contain "S.D.G." markings, and many (about 35 percent) contain both.

Within each of these periods in Bach's career, it happens that the usage percentages for the various markings in his large-scale secular vocal compositions and in his collections of instrumental pieces are not definingly different from what they are for his church compositions. (Note that throughout Bach's career, no chamber compositions or individual solo pieces, whether liturgical or secular, contain the markings.)

Bach's employment of these notational practices cannot have been simply conventional (analogous, for example, to the commonplace and by-and-large perfunctory action of saying "Bless you" or "God bless you" when someone sneezes). Had it been so, we would have expected to encounter the notations either randomly, or almost everywhere in Bach scores, or almost never, or somewhere in between but always at more or less the same level of frequency.

The striking patterns of Bach's notations suggest, then, that for much of his composing career—at least regarding his larger-scale individual compositions and his collections of pieces, secular or liturgical—Bach often truly did seek divine help in starting his scores and somewhat less often truly did offer forth divine praise in completing them.

From a properly informed consideration of Bach's notational practice, we are given—against the drift on this question from Butt's important essay—no hint that Bach thought of himself as a secular, "modern" artist.

It is true that during the 1740s, Bach appears, through his various frustrations with the authorities, to have lost nearly all interest in his tasks as director of church music in Leipzig,[15] but the continuing pattern of devotional markings in his scores from that period appear to indicate that he had not lost interest in his traditional Lutheranism. Further evidence of Bach's serious ongoing interest in Martin Luther and God lies in the fact that in the 1740s, he purchased another (massive) set of Luther's collected writings in German and, moreover, in the fact that at this time, he made a series of handwritten theological annotations in the margins of his Calov Bible.[16]

With regard specifically to Bach's "S.D.G." markings and their notion that honor belongs to God alone, it is worth mentioning that the following passage from the commentary on Ecclesiastes 1:14 was highlighted, apparently by Bach (and presumably not for disapproval), in his Calov Bible:

---

[15] See Michael Maul, "'Having to Perform and Direct the Music in the Capellmeister's Stead for Two Whole Years': Observations on How Bach Understood His Post during the 1740s," *Understanding Bach* 12 (2017): 37–58.

[16] A facsimile of Bach's book-auction receipt is printed in Leaver, *Bachs theologische Bibliothek*, 42. On the late dating of Bach's marginalia in Calov, see Hans-Joachim Schulze, ed., *Bach-Dokumente III* (Kassel: Bärenreiter, 1972), 636–637; see also Schulze's further findings as reported in Howard H. Cox, ed., *The Calov Bible of J. S. Bach* (Ann Arbor, MI: UMI Research Press, 1985). In addition, some ten years ago on eBay, a "Merian [Illustrated] Bible" surfaced whose title-page inscription, "JSBach. / 1744," was verified as Bach's handwriting by Peter Wollny of the Bach Archive in Leipzig.

12 CONSTRAINTS OF HISTORY ON INTERPRETATION

As soon as we humans do a bit well in an enterprise, from that hour forth we want to have the honor; a greedy desire for honor soon stirs within us. We think, "this is my doing—for this the land and its people have me to thank," and immediately we grab for the praise which solely and purely belongs to God.[17]

Exalting Human Reason?

Exalting reason above revelation (however flawed reason might be) as an arbiter of truth, including in religion, theology, and morality, is a hallmark of the modern. Remarkably, every one of Bach's vocal compositions that touches on reason rails against it as worse than useless in spiritual matters, and his music appears to be, in that sense, quintessentially anti-modern. One thus readily imagines, for example, the renowned Leipzig power couple Luise and Johann Christoph Gottsched—along with any others among their fellow members of Bach's congregations who were followers of the rationalist "new philosophy" of Gottfried Wilhelm Leibniz and Christian Wolff—continually shaking their heads at the sentiments expressed in Bach's cantatas.

Perhaps the textually and musically most forceful (and entertaining) of the anti-reason examples in Bach is the tenor aria from his church cantata *Wo Gott der Herr nicht bei uns hält* (BWV 178), the beginning of whose text reads: "Shut up, just shut up, *tottery reason!*"[18]

---

[17] Calov, *Die heilige Bibel*, II:1056: "Albald uns Menschen ein wenig ein Anschlag geräth / von Stund an wollen wir die Ehre haben / bald reget sich bey uns der Ehrgeitz / dencken / das habe ich gethan / das haben Land und Leute mir zu dancken / und greiffen alsobald nach dem Ruhm / welcher alleine und reine GOTT gehöret."

[18] I recommend especially the scathing 1988 recording on Teldec by Kurt Equiluz with the Concentus Musicus Wien, directed by Nikolaus Harnoncourt, *Bach: Cantatas, Vol. 41 (BWV 175–179)*. See also the marvelous discussion of this cantata and its performance by Harnoncourt in Richard Taruskin, "Facing Up, Finally, to Bach's Dark Vision," in *Text and Act: Essays on Music and Performance*, by Richard Taruskin (New York: Oxford University Press, 1995), 312–313.

BACH AGAINST MODERNITY   13

Here is a chronological survey of all the appearances that reason makes (namely, from 1714 to 1736/37) in Bach's extant vocal compositions:[19]

> BWV 152/5: *reason*—the blind leader—seduces
> BWV 76/5: Christ is the light [illuminating, here, the darkness] of *reason*
> BWV 186/3: do not let *reason* ensnare you: your Helper, Jacob's light, you can see in scripture
> BWV 178/6: tottery *reason*
> BWV 178/7: *reason*—an enemy, who will not be trusted in the future—fights with sword against faith
> BWV 180/4: *reason* does not help; only God's spirit can teach us through his Word
> BWV 175/5: blinded *reason*
> BWV 2/2: foolish *reason*, instead of the Bible, is their guide
> BWV 35/3: if I contemplate you, you precious Son of God, then *reason* and also understanding flee therefrom
> BWV 213/2: *reason* demands that I [Hercules] chase after all these things: virtue, brilliance, and glory, and majesty
> BWV 197/2: what *reason* regards as impossible, does come about with God

I do not see or hear anything in Bach's musical settings to suggest that these vocal compositions subvert their anti-Enlightenment messages at the same time that they enunciate them.

In principle, Bach could have held other views than those expressed in his music—it is theoretically (if remotely) possible

---

[19] See also Eric T. Chafe, *Tonal Allegory in the Vocal Music of J. S. Bach* (Berkeley: University of California Press, 1991), 224–253. Regarding contemporary assessment (by, e.g., the Gottscheds) of Bach's music in general as strongly anti-rationalist, see Andrew Talle, *Beyond Bach: Music and Everyday Life in the Eighteenth Century* (Urbana-Champaign: University of Illinois Press, 2017), 126–133.

14   CONSTRAINTS OF HISTORY ON INTERPRETATION

that Bach himself had a high spiritual view of reason but harangued against it with his music only to please his conservative employers.

As it happens, though, one can document something of what Bach's private views would likely have been by studying his private annotations in the Calov Study Bible from his personal library.

I will focus briefly on Bach's encounter with Calov's citation of Luther's comments regarding the fall into sin at Genesis 3:6–7, which for Lutheran orthodoxy was one of the most important passages in the Bible.[20] This will serve to show how in conservative Lutheranism, it would have been structurally impossible to take a positive view of the human endowment of reason in spiritual matters.[21] The italics in the following excerpt indicate text that was handwritten into the margin by Bach, as Calov had inadvertently skipped over those words in quoting Luther:

> The scholastics, says he [i.e., says Luther], contend that the righteousness Adam was created with will not have been in Adam's nature, but rather was just like an ornament or gift with which humankind will, at first, have been adorned, as when one sets a wreath on a beautiful young unmarried woman, which wreath is not part of the nature of the young woman but rather is something extraordinary and separate from her nature *that comes along from outside, and—without impact on the* [young woman's] *nature*—can be taken away again. . . . But against such teaching, because it slights Original Sin, one must be on guard, like against poison. . . . Our naturalia [which do include—as Luther says in the same passage—"righteousness, and reason"] . . . are, through

---

[20] See, e.g., Martin Luther, "The Smalcald Articles of Christian Doctrine (1537)," trans. William Russell, in *The Book of Concord: The Confessions of the Evangelical Lutheran Church*, ed. Robert Kolb and Timothy J. Wengert (Minneapolis: Fortress, 2000), 310–311.

[21] The discussion of this passage from Calov in Butt, *Bach's Dialogue with Modernity*, 53, has the Lutheran understanding of natural human endowments the wrong way around and does not include Calov's quoting of Luther's significant attendant comments on reason. The full passages are given in Robin A. Leaver, *J. S. Bach and Scripture* (St. Louis, MO: Concordia, 1985), 57–58.

BACH AGAINST MODERNITY 15

sin, disarranged and corrupted.... This poison [of what Luther in this same passage calls the "frightful, heavy sins of humankind"] is after this manner so widely percolated through the flesh, body, and soul—[and] the will, the intellect, and reason—that not only can one not extract it, but also [it] is not recognized as being sin.[22]

The content of Bach's encounter with Luther's comments on natural human endowments helps us greatly to understand the dim view of reason expressed in Bach's church cantatas.

I am not suggesting that in writing his vocal compositions Bach was directly influenced by his reading of Calov. I am simply suggesting that his documented reading of Calov provides evidence of his private engagement with the theological and other issues that were also addressed in his public vocal compositions.

It is striking that the sentiments expressed in Bach's vocal music are continually paralleled in his Calov notations. Most of Bach's vocal music was composed from the 1710s to the 1730s, whereas his Calov notations were entered in the 1730s and 1740s. In view of the fact that almost all the private notations came not before but well after the public compositions (and thus the notations cannot be simply written off as Bach engaging in disinterested research to meet his liturgical duties), we can logically infer that Bach did subscribe to the sentiments expressed in his vocal music.[23]

---

[22] Calov, *Die heilige Bibel*, I:32–33: "Die Schul-Lehrer / sagt er / *disputi*ren / dass die Gerechtigkeit / darin Adam erschaffen ist / nicht sey gewest in Adams Natur / sondern sey gleich wie ein Schmuck oder Gabe gewest / damit der Mensch erstlich sey gezieret worden / als wenn man einer schönen Jungfrau einen Krantz auffsetzt / welcher Krantz nicht ein Theil der Natur ist der Jungfrauen / sondern ist etwas sonderliches und abgeschiedenes von der Natur [*das von aussen hinzu kömmt, u. ohne Verletzung der Natur*] wieder kan abgethan werden.... Aber für solcher Lehre / weil sie die Erbsünde gering macht / soll man sich hüten / wie für einem Gifft.... [D]ie *Naturalia* ... durch die Sünde verruckt und verderbet seyn.... Diese Gifft so weit durchs Fleisch / Leib / und Seele / [und] durch den Willen / Verstand / und Vernunfft also durchgegossen ist / dass man sie nicht allein nicht herauss nehmen kan / sondern wird auch nicht für Sünde erkandt."

[23] On this point, see also Michael Marissen, "Bach Was Far More Religious Than You Might Think," *New York Times*, Sunday Arts & Leisure section, April 1, 2018, AR10.

16 CONSTRAINTS OF HISTORY ON INTERPRETATION

Righteousness and reason, then, according to orthodox Lutheranism, are not adornments but are part of the nature of what a person is. Through the fall of Adam and Eve into sin, however, these naturalia have been "corrupted," and thus, humans, on their own, are incapable of being truly righteous or truly reasonable.

As a result of the fall, human reason became "dark." Only God can illuminate it (see, e.g., the expressions in Bach's Cantatas 76 and 186 that were previously given)—human reason, in Luther's famous formulation, is a "blind whore."

No wonder Bach's vocal compositions express only contempt for reason.

Exalting Human Achievement and Good Works?

Considering that one encounters nothing but negative assessment in the various Bach vocal compositions that mention reason, it should come as no surprise that his music also reflects and promotes an unfavorable estimation of human achievement and that in this way, too, the repertory is decidedly anti-modern.

Consider, as a particularly good example, the run of the alto recitative and bass aria from Bach's church cantata *Ach wie flüchtig, ach wie nichtig* (BWV 26)—whose musical setting in the bass aria is a sort of bourrée-from-hell:

> *Recit*
> Joy will turn into sadness;
> Beauty withers like a flower;
> The greatest strength will become weakened;
> Fortune, it shifts with time;
> Soon it is over and done with honor and glory;
> Knowledge and whatever a *human* being *fashions*
> Will in the end be destroyed by the grave.

> *Aria*
> To set one's heart on earthly treasures
> Is a seduction of the foolish world. . . .[24]

The German of the recitative's closing couplet—"Die Wissenschaft und was ein Mensche dichtet, / Wird endlich durch das Grab vernichtet"—has proven linguistically confusing for many, including for Germans. Some understand it to mean something along the lines of either "Scholarship, and the poetry a person creates, / Are finally made futile by the grave" or "Learning, and the writings of humans, / Are canceled in the end by the grave."

But the verb *dichten* here does not refer specifically to writings and poetry. Cantata 26 is plainly alluding to the language of an extremely prominent verse in the German Bible, namely, Genesis 8:21, rendered by Luther as "Das *Dichten* des *menschlichen* Herzens ist böse von Jugend auf" ("The *fashioning* of the *human* heart is evil, from youth onward"). Poetry is, to be sure, a type of *dichten*, in that it involves the fashioning of words.[25] But "das menschliche Dichten" in Luther's Bible and "was ein Mensche dichtet" in Bach's cantata both refer more generally to all human fashioning, of any sort.

Note, too, that in older German, the word *Wissenschaft* refers to human knowledge in general, of any type—it does not necessarily refer specifically to "science," "scholarship," or "advanced learning."

Should it happen that humans fashion anything worthwhile and even should they perform countless good works, the harsh reality, according to the orthodox Lutheranism reflected and promoted in

---

[24] *Recit*: "Die Freude wird zur Traurigkeit, / Die Schönheit fällt als eine Blume, / Die grösste Stärke wird geschwächt, / Es ändert sich das Glücke mit der Zeit, / Bald ist es aus mit Ehr und Ruhme, / Die Wissenschaft und was ein Mensche dichtet, / Wird endlich durch das Grab vernichtet." *Aria*: "An irdische Schätze das Herze zu hängen, / Ist eine Verführung der törichten Welt." The librettist for this cantata, as with nearly all of Bach's vocal compositions, is unknown. (All translations of German text in this chapter are my own.)

[25] As it happens, the word "poetry" is ultimately derived from the ancient Greek word *poesis*, "to make, create, produce."

18   CONSTRAINTS OF HISTORY ON INTERPRETATION

Bach's church cantatas, is that in the end, people are either going to be eternally "saved" or "condemned," and no human endeavor will do anything to justify a person for God's salvation; "faith alone" (itself an unmerited gift from God) is what "justifies."

The standard Lutheran notions about good works and justification by faith alone are laid out straightforwardly in the bass recitative and aria from Bach's church cantata *Wer da gläubet und getauft wird* (BWV 37), given here with italics for emphasis:

> *Recit*
> You mortals, do you desire
> To look upon
> God's countenance with me?
> Then [you need to understand that] *you cannot bank
>   on good works;*
> For though a Christian must, without a doubt,
> Practice good works
> (Because it is the severe will of God),
> Yet *faith alone is what makes it such
> That before God we are justified* [for salvation] *and*
>   [eternally] *blessed.*
>
> *Aria*
> Faith provides wings to the soul,
> [So] that it [the soul] soars into heaven . . .[26]

As far as I can see, modernity's notions that humans, on their own, can truly make the world better and can truly make themselves

---

[26] *Recit*: "Ihr Sterblichen, verlanget ihr, / Mit mir / Das Antlitz Gottes anzuschauen? / So dürft ihr nicht auf gute Werke bauen; / Denn ob sich wohl ein Christ / Muss in den guten Werken üben, / Weil es der ernste Wille Gottes ist, / So macht der Glaube doch allein, / Dass wir vor Gott gerecht und selig sein." *Aria*: "Der Glaube schafft der Seele Flügel, / Dass sie sich in den Himmel schwingt . . ."

BACH AGAINST MODERNITY   19

better are entirely foreign to the sentiments expressed verbally and musically throughout both the public Bach and the private Bach.[27]

Exalting Religious Tolerance?

A high percentage of the theological books that Bach owned were polemical in nature,[28] and there is at least some specific documentary evidence, as we will see below, that he was interested in such material and did read it.

Religious *contempt*—as opposed to religious *disagreement*—in Bach is a prickly and sensitive issue these days. Two standard responses have been to trivialize the level of prejudice (and those who call attention to it) or to deny its existence altogether. I will leave aside the trivializing approach and focus on an instructive example of the denial.

After a brouhaha surrounding a recent museum exhibition in Eisenach, Germany, on Bach and prejudice, I was told the following in an email message from a friend in Leipzig who is an extremely prominent figure in the world of Bach and religion:

---

[27] Butt, *Bach's Dialogue with Modernity*, 56–57 and passim, reports Bach's having collected "many [Lutheran writings] of a more obviously 'modern' mindset" and speaks of mystically minded Lutherans feeling "encouraged to draw closer to a works-oriented confessionalism" and also suggests that Bach had significant partial sympathies with Pietism, which is said to have had a "works-oriented justification." These are serious misunderstandings of Lutheran theology. The more radical types of Lutheranism did feature many nontrivial differences from orthodox Lutheranism, and the former certainly did place greater emphasis, for example, on the earthly virtues of better moral behavior and of increased charitable work. But even though each group accused the others of all manner of doctrinal and further lapses, every group in the Lutheran spectrum always insisted that humans can expect either a blessed or an accursed afterlife and that they are justified for salvation by faith alone through grace alone. On the enduring foundational role of grace (over good works) in Pietism's understanding of salvation, see, e.g., Richard L. Gawthrop, *Pietism and the Making of Eighteenth-Century Prussia* (Cambridge: Cambridge University Press, 1993), 96, 110, 140–149, 152–154, 205–207.

[28] Listed in Leaver, *Bachs theologische Bibliothek*, 193.

20 CONSTRAINTS OF HISTORY ON INTERPRETATION

Bach's music does not lend itself to insulting particular groups of people. Whoever sings Bach cannot be hostile to "others." It is significant that in times of social crisis the music of Bach has been, and is, understood as a clear vote for peace, for human dignity, for protection.

What is being professed here is that Bach was, and is, one fantastic modern liberal! Though each of my friend's three claims is either an obvious falsehood or an interpretive lapse, I will attend to just the first, which is an obvious falsehood.

When I had coffee in Leipzig with this friend soon after our email exchange, I ventured in our follow-up discussion that it seemed pretty clear to me that Bach's music sometimes does lend itself, rather well, to insulting particular groups of people. I gave as prime examples Bach's Cantatas 18 and 126.

Cantata 18, *Gleichwie der Regen und Schnee vom Himmel fällt*, includes the following prayer: "And in the face *of the Muslim's and of the Pope's fierce murderousness* and *blasphemies, outrages, and rantings*, protect us in a fatherly manner. Hear us, dear Lord God!"[29] Similarly, Cantata 126, *Erhalt uns, Herr, bei deinem Wort*, opens with the first stanza from a famous hymn of Luther's:

> Uphold us, Lord, with your word,
> And restrain *the murderousness of the Pope and of the Muslim*,
> [These] who want to topple Jesus Christ, your Son,
> From his throne![30]

(By the way, it is the hymn's "murderousness *of the Pope*" that Bach's musical setting emphasizes.)

"No, no," my friend condescended to explain:

---

[29] "Und uns für des Türken und des Pabsts grausamen Mord und Lästerungen, Wüten und Toben, väterlich behüten. Erhör uns, lieber Herre Gott!"

[30] "Erhalt uns, Herr, bei deinem Wort / Und steur des Papsts und Türken Mord, / Die Jesum Christum, deinen Sohn, / Stürzen wollen von seinen Thron!"

everyone in the Lutheran churches, then as now, has always understood these expressions to be the merely "historical" language of the early Reformation. The "Pope-and-Turk" when it later appears in Bach's cantata refers, for his listeners, only to *generalized* enemies, not to Catholics or Muslims or any other particular group. And anyway Bach had no choice but to set these texts as given to him.

Over and over in my career as a student of Bach's music, I have heard dodgy statements like this one from personages high and low, and so I do, alas, see great value in spending some time countering them rather vigorously here.

The issue at hand, I responded for a start, was not whether Bach had any choice in setting his texts. The question was whether any of the texts that Bach did set, whatever the circumstances, do lend themselves to insulting particular groups of people.

I went on to say that any claim about post-Reformation Lutherans always (or even by and large) not taking the hymn's "Pope and Turk" as referring to Catholics and Muslims is radically unsustainable.

For example, already in Bach's day, line 2 from *Erhalt uns, Herr* was given in some Lutheran hymnals with its now-standard post-Reformation textual variant, "and restrain the murderousness *of your enemies.*"[31] Evidently, some Lutherans had become troubled about the fact that Luther's original text sounded unseemly, in that its explicit language *was* understood as referring to Catholics and Muslims/Turks.

We know, too, that Lutherans in Bach's Leipzig were well aware of what were considered to be real problems surrounding this hymn. For the festive services marking the celebration in 1739 of the two-hundredth anniversary of the coming of the Reformation to Leipzig, the elector of Saxony (who, though himself a convert

---

[31] "Und steure deiner Feinde Mord."

22 CONSTRAINTS OF HISTORY ON INTERPRETATION

to Roman Catholicism, remained the head of the Saxon Lutheran church) issued the express directive that *Erhalt uns, Herr* was not to be sung in the churches. In clear defiance, the Leipzigers went ahead and included this hymn in their services.

For the celebration in 1755 of the two-hundredth anniversary of the Religious Peace of Augsburg (a treaty marking Catholicism's political acceptance of Lutheranism), again there were directives from on high to keep things friendly and pleasant. And what did the Leipzigers bring out for their church cantata on this meant-to-be ecumenical occasion but—in a massive affront—a work (Bach's?) entitled *Uphold Us, Lord, With Your Word, and Restrain the Murderousness of the Pope and of the Muslim.*[32]

Today, too, the "murderousness of the Pope and Turk" is clearly not understood by everyone in the Lutheran churches as mere "historical language."

In the main text of the recently published urtext score of Cantata 126 from the Carus-Verlag (whose performing materials are widely used in the church and the concert hall), the editor has printed our hymn with its more irenical post-Reformation textual variant, not with the polemical wording that appears in the Bach sources.[33]

Likewise, present-day Lutherans in the Bach city of Leipzig certainly do not understand the libretto of Cantata 126 as mere historical language. For example, in a recent rendering of this cantata, on January 30, 2016, in the Thomaskirche, the cleaned-up text

---

[32] On the inclusion of *Erhalt uns, Herr* in these Leipzig celebrations of 1739 and 1755, see Michael Maul, "Der 200. Jahrestag des Augsburger Religionsfriedens (1755) und die Leipziger Bach-Pflege in der zweiten Hälfte des 18. Jh.," *Bach-Jahrbuch* 86 (2000): 101–118. The libretto of the 1755 cantata performed in Leipzig was printed in H. E. Schwartze, *Vollständige Jubelacten des . . . Religionsfriedens- und Freudenfestes der Evangelischen Kirche* (Leipzig, 1756), 105–106; for a facsimile of this extract, see Maul, "Der 200. Jahrestag," 107.

[33] Johann Sebastian Bach, *Erhalt uns, Herr, bei deinem Wort, BWV 126*, ed. Karin Wollschläger, Stuttgarter Bach-Ausgaben: Urtext (Stuttgart: Carus-Verlag, 2012); the wording Bach employed is indicated in a footnote.

BACH AGAINST MODERNITY   23

was sung and printed,[34] not the one Bach used, and much of the preacher's accompanying address was devoted to rueing the infamous original language of *Erhalt uns, Herr*, deeming it "in no way harmless."[35]

Bach himself owned a fair amount of contemptuous anti-Catholic literature, most notably Philipp Jacob Spener's *Gerechter Eifer wider das Antichristische Pabstthum* but also the Jena and Altenburg editions of Luther's notorious *Wider das Papsttum zu Rom, vom Teufel gestiftet.*

Some of this very material was highlighted, apparently by Bach (and presumably not for disapproval), in his Calov Bible at the commentary on Matthew 18:17, where Calov quoted the following from Luther's *Wider das Papsttum* (emphasis mine):

> Herr Luther, Altenburg Edition, vol. 8, p. 458: . . . Here is demanded not only of the Church . . . but also of you and me, that *we should* judge, convict, and *damn the Pope* with a verdict as a . . . heathen and tax-collector. For he will not hear . . . *how he rants* via many decrees and decretal epistles, . . . intending thereby . . . *to force Christians* obediently to carry out, to laud, and *to worship* as a divine truth *such atrocity.*[36]

Bach likewise owned the Jena and Altenburg editions of Luther's contemptuous anti-Muslim treatise, *Vermahnung zum Gebet wider den Türken.*

---

[34] The printed program was posted at www.mvmc.de/motette and can be found in the site's archives.

[35] The preacher's remarks were posted at https://www.thomaskirche.org/r-2016-motetten-a-7548.html; no longer available.

[36] Calov, *Die heilige Bibel*, V:182: "Hr. Lutherus Tom.IIX. Altenb[urger Ausgabe]. p. 458. . . . Hie wird nicht allein der Kirchen / . . . sondern auch dir und mir geboten / dass wir den Pabst sollen richten / verurtheilen / und verdammen / mit einem Urtheil / als . . . Heyde und Zöllner. Denn er wil nicht hören . . . / wie er tobet durch viel Decret und Decretal / wil dazu . . . die Christen zwingen / solche Greuel Gehorsam zu leisten / zu loben und anzubeten / als eine Göttliche Warheit."

24 CONSTRAINTS OF HISTORY ON INTERPRETATION

My Leipzig interlocutor assured me, now with apodictic certainty in his voice, that "Bach himself could not have had any interest *whatsoever* in anti-Muslim sentiment." But the Bach documents do not support this notion, either. Bach appears, for example, to have read the anti-Muslim comments in his Calov Bible at Daniel 7:25 with at least some interest, highlighting them with "NB" (presumably not with the idea of indicating dissent):

> But the law [will be—blasphemously—changed, under the "Fourth Beast"] through the Koran, as imposed by the accursed Muhammad, elevating his doctrine over the law of Moses and Christ. [here Bach wrote "NB" in the margin][37] . . . It will be some 1277½ years that the Muhammadan empire shall stand, . . . such that only 211 years still remain from this, the 1679th year of Christ.[38]

Is any of this contempt surprising? No, it is not surprising (or at least, it should not be) that people in Luther's and Bach's days could be so religiously intolerant.[39] But it is surprising (or at least, it ought to be) that today there are so many intelligent and decent people like my Leipzig friend who cling to modern views of Bach and his output that are patently contradicted by all available evidence, both repertorial and biographical.

---

[37] Of this "NB," Cox wrote (having conferred with Hans-Joachim Schulze of the Bach-Archiv Leipzig), "We can say confidently that it is from Bach's hand." Cox, *The Calov Bible*, 24.

[38] Calov, *Die heilige Bibel*, III:982: "Das Gesetz aber durch den Alcoran / so der verfluchte Mahomet eingeführet / und über Moses und Christi Gesetz seine Lehre erhoben. . . . [S]inds etwa 1277½ / dass so lang das Mahomerische Reich stehen sol / . . . dass nur noch 211. Jahr übrig von diesen 1679sten Jahr Christi."

[39] By contrast, however, it is worth noting, for example, that in the 1720s, Johann Christoph Gottsched delivered a speech in Leipzig on the beneficial tolerance of all religions; see Talle, *Beyond Bach*, 113.

Chauvinism in Bach?

I am not aware of any outright jingoism in Bach, but the few references to good citizenship that come up in the vocal repertory certainly are far from "cosmopolitan."

Consider, for example, the opening movement from Bach's church cantata *Ein ungefärbt Gemüte* (BWV 24):

> An unfeigned disposition
> To [variably, "of"] *German* faithfulness and goodness
> Makes us lovely before God and humanity.
> > Christians' doings and dealings,
> > Their entire way of life
> > Should stand on this same footing.[40]

When I suggested in a recent church-basement lecture that this aria text and its delightful and rather upbeat and insistent musical setting were somewhat chauvinistic, an audience member took great umbrage, arguing that "*German* faithfulness and goodness" means nothing but "*everyday* faithfulness and goodness."

I responded that this would be like arguing that "I got *gypped*" means nothing but "I got *cheated*." Does not saying "I got gypped"—whatever the speaker's intentions—also imply that the so-called gypsies are more likely to cheat than many others? Similarly, does not our Cantata 24 aria imply that Germans are at least somewhat more likely than many others to be faithful and good, and is not this notion indeed cheerfully reinforced by the whole of the aria's B section, which proclaims that Christians' *entire way of life* should stand on this same footing?[41]

---

[40] "Ein ungefärbt Gemüte / An [bzw., 'Von'] deutscher Treu und Güte / Macht uns vor Gott und Menschen schön. / Der Christen Tun und Handel, / Ihr ganzer Lebenswandel / Soll auf dergleichen Fusse stehn."

[41] Martin Petzoldt comments that "today, the talk [in Bach's Cantata 24] of 'German faithfulness and goodness' may prove itself to be an impediment," but "in the time of Bach such a designation is still far removed from the nationalistic undertones of

26 CONSTRAINTS OF HISTORY ON INTERPRETATION

Bach the Progressive?

The current *Oxford English Dictionary* defines (with quotations from the nineteenth to the twenty-first centuries) the noun *progressive* thus: "A person holding progressive, avant-garde, or liberal views; an advocate or supporter of social, religious, or political progress or reform, or of change within or to a particular political system."

Bach's vocal compositions most certainly do *not* give expression to socially, religiously, or politically progressive sentiments.[42]

The classic premodern, hierarchical social view that was maintained by traditional Lutheranism is laid out clearly, and with some musical animation, for example, at line 6 in the bass recitative from Bach's church cantata *Nur jedem das Seine* (BWV 163):

> You are, my God, the giver of all gifts;
> We have what we have
> From your hand alone.
> You, you have given us
> Spirit, soul, body, and life,
> And goods and chattel, and *honor and station!*[43]

Similarly, a crystal-clear passage discussing this issue of station was highlighted, apparently by Bach (and presumably not for

---

the nineteenth century." Petzoldt sanguinely concludes, "Within the text set by Bach, 'German faithfulness and goodness' denotes 'speaking with anyone sans circumlocution'; the designation [simply] means: practicing undisguised faithfulness and goodness." Martin Petzoldt, *Bach-Kommentar: Theologisch-musikwissenschaftliche Kommentierung der geistlichen Vokalwerke Johann Sebastian Bachs* (Kassel: Bärenreiter, 2004–2019), 1:101.

[42] For a discussion of the apparent social conservatism likewise of instrumental compositions by Bach, see Marissen, *The Social and Religious Designs*, esp. 111–119.

[43] "Du bist, mein Gott, der Geber aller Gaben; / Wir haben, was wir haben, / Allein von deiner Hand. / Du, du hast uns gegeben / Geist, Seele, Leib und Leben / Und Hab und Gut und Ehr und Stand!"

disapproval), in his Calov Bible at the commentary on Ecclesiastes 6:7, where Calov reported:

> In German we say, "*Each one has his appointed portion*: God has distributed to each one his portion." Magistracy has its labor; subjects have their labor. The man has his labor; women, children also have their labor. To burghers, peasants, common people God gives common labor; but upon princes, lords, great potentates he imposes great things, great dealings, that they have enough to take up.[44]

In connection with this point, it is worth noting that in his many troubles with his superiors, Bach never gave any hint that he ought to be appreciated and recognized for his artistic talents rather than for his official position in the God-given, biblically revealed vocational hierarchy. What Bach persistently argued was that others had improperly assumed the prerogatives that went with his station. (There is no evidence to suggest that this was simply Bach's disingenuous, calculated strategy for arguing with his hidebound, unmusical employers.)[45]

God and King in Bach

We can come to a close by bringing virtually all of the anti-modern strands of our discussion together in a brief consideration of God and royalty in Bach.

---

[44] Calov, *Die heilige Bibel*, II:1094: "wir auf Teutsch sprechen: Ein ieglicher hat sein bescheiden Theil: Einem ieglichen hat GOtt sein Theil abgemessen / Obrigkeit hat ihre Arbeit / Unterthanen haben ihre Arbeit / der Mann hat seine Arbeit / Weiber / Kinder haben auch ihre Arbeit / Bürgern / Bauren / gemeinen Leuten gibt GOtt gemeine Arbeit / aber Fürsten/ Herren / grossen Potentaten leget er grosse Sachen / grosse Händel auff / dass sie zutragen gnug haben."

[45] See, e.g., Denis Arnold, *Bach* (New York: Oxford University Press, 1984), 58–59.

28   CONSTRAINTS OF HISTORY ON INTERPRETATION

Many Bach lovers, I have discovered, are convinced that Bach's secular cantatas are free from what they consider theological baggage, apparently unaware that God is explicitly mentioned often enough in this repertory. These Bach lovers are certainly unaware that significant biblical language is often lurking about in there as well.

Consider, as an example for Bach's setting of typically undetected biblical language, the closing chorus from his magnificent secular cantata *Preise dein Glücke, gesegnetes Sachsen* (BWV 215):

[O *God*, who is the] Founder of the realms, Lord and Master of
the crowns—
Build up the throne[46] that August [the elector of Saxony and
king of Poland] occupies!
Deck out his dynasty
With imperishable thriving!
Let us inhabit in peace the lands
That he [August—but only by God's bestowal] with *justice and
with mercy* protects.[47]

The cantata assumes a familiarity with the language of God's granting specifically of "Gnade und Recht" (mercy and justice) to rulers like King David of Israel, as explicitly proclaimed with those very words in Psalm 101:1.

The gloss at Psalm 101:2 in Bach's Calov Bible is extremely illuminating for his secular cantatas, and this bit of its commentary (given here in italics) was partly highlighted, apparently by Bach (and presumably not to register disapproval):

---

[46] Alluding to Psalm 89:4, "I [God] will, ever and ever, build up your throne [*deinen Stuhl bauen für und für*]."

[47] "Stifter der Reiche, Beherrscher der Kronen, / Baue den Thron, den Augustus besitzt! / Ziere sein Haus / Mit unvergänglichem Wohlergehn aus! / Lass uns die Länder in Friede bewohnen, / Die er mit Recht und mit Gnade beschützt."

BACH AGAINST MODERNITY   29

I [King David] deal circumspectly and fairly with those who belong to me.... *Herr Luther explains it thus:... For such seriousness
and deeds* [as King David's] *are part of neither reason nor natural
law.*[48] [The following sentence is underlined:] *But wherever there
is a king or a prince or a nobleman who with seriousness (yes, with
seriousness, I say) attends to God and his Word, these you may well
hold as God's prodigies, and these you may well call rare game in
the kingdom of heaven. For they do such things not from reason, or
from lofty wisdom—rather, God stirs their heart.*[49]

Cantata 215's lauded ruler, it appears, protects his subjects with
God-given mercy and justice,[50] not as an "enlightened despot"; and
this ruler operates not out of human reason and natural law, but out
of the revealed Word of God and divine positive law; furthermore,
unlike with enlightened rulers, this king is believed to be author-
ized not by the people but by God. As far as I can tell, there are no
countervailing views of royalty to be found in the Bach repertory.

One of the greatest musical moments in all of Bach, I think,
and I feel sure most readers will agree, is the opening chorus from
Cantata 215, which explicitly acknowledges God as the upholder of
the Saxon throne:

> Praise your good fortune, blessed Saxony,
> Since *God* upholds the throne of your king.[51]

---

[48] That is, a notion of law as made up of inherent rights (as distinguished from divine
positive law, whose content is determined by the will of God).

[49] Calov, *Die heilige Bibel*, II:653: "Ich handele fürsichtig und redlich bey denen / die
mir zugehören. . . . Herr Lutherus erklärets also: . . . Denn solcher Ernst und Thaten
stecken nicht in der Vernunfft / noch im natürlichen Recht. Wo aber ein König oder
Fürst / oder Adel ist / die sich mit Ernst / ja mit Ernst / sag ich / umb Gott und sein Wort
annemen / die magstu wol für Wunderleute Gottes halten / und seltzam Wildpret im
Himmelreich heissen. Denn sie thun solches nicht aus Vernunfft / oder hoher Weisheit /
sondern Gott rühret ihr Hertz."

[50] The same was said of Prince Leopold of Anhalt-Köthen at the sixth movement from
the birthday cantata *Lobet den Herrn, alle seine Heerscharen* (BWV 1147).

[51] "Preise dein Glücke, gesegnetes Sachsen, / Weil Gott den Thron deines Königs
erhält."

30 CONSTRAINTS OF HISTORY ON INTERPRETATION

This music somehow sounds even more glorious, I am sure most will also agree, in its setting of the following royal text from Bach's *Mass in B minor*: "Hosanna in the highest [to king Jesus, who comes in the name of the Lord]."

The "secular" Bach and the "sacred" Bach, it seems, are one.

Envoi

Despite so much recent scholarly and journalistic or devotional talk of Bach's music as completely "transcending its epoch," as being "enlightened," or as being "progressive," and despite the remarkably wide appeal of Bach's music among today's expert and general publics, the unsettling difficulty I am left with is this: All things considered, what basis is there for believing that Bach was, and is, in any way a *modern* figure?

While we are arguably free to make use of Bach and his music in whatever historically informed or uninformed ways we find fitting,[52] we ought, I submit, also to be on the ethical alert for a kind of cultural narcissism in which we end up miscasting Bach in our own ideological image and proclaiming the authenticity of that image, and hence its prestige value, in support of our own agendas.

---

[52] One must, of course, beware of the "genetic fallacy," but what is less often understood or acknowledged is the need to watch out for what might be called the "fallacy of reception," the notion that an interpretation has to be considered warranted simply by dint of the fact that it is felt to work so well for one's purposes.

2

Bach's Handwritten Entries in His Bible

Bach biographers do not have it easy. Has there ever been a composer who wrote so much extraordinary music and left so little documentation of his personal life? Life-writing abhors a vacuum, and experts have indulged in all manner of speculation, generally mirroring their own approaches to the world, about how Bach must have understood himself and his works. A current fancy is that Bach was more of a forward-looking, quasi-scientific thinker than a traditional orthodox Lutheran believer.[1]

In arriving at this view, scholars have either ignored, underestimated, or misinterpreted a rich source of evidence: Bach's personal three-volume Study Bible, extensively marked with his own notations. Bach's copy of these tomes, published in 1681–1682 and consisting of scriptural text with commentary from Luther's sermons and other writings assembled by Abraham Calov, was unexpectedly discovered in the 1930s among the belongings of a German immigrant family in Frankenmuth, Michigan,[2] and is housed today at Concordia Seminary Library in St. Louis, Missouri.[3]

---

[1] See esp. Butt, *Bach's Dialogue with Modernity*; Christoph Wolff, *Johann Sebastian Bach: The Learned Musician—Updated Edition* (New York: W. W. Norton, 2013).

[2] The best-researched and fullest telling of the story is Mark W. Knoll, "Leonard Reichle and J. S. Bach's Bible in Frankenmuth, Michigan," in *Er ist der Vater, wir sind die Bub'n: Essays in Honor of Christoph Wolff*, ed. Paul Corneilson and Peter Wollny (Ann Arbor, MI: Steglein, 2010), 207–224.

[3] Calov, *Die heilige Bibel*. Bach's exemplar was printed as a color facsimile in 2017 by the Uitgeverij van Wijnen in Franeker, Netherlands.

Bach against Modernity. Michael Marissen, Oxford University Press. © Oxford University Press 2023.
DOI: 10.1093/oso/9780197669495.003.0002

32 CONSTRAINTS OF HISTORY ON INTERPRETATION

All three volumes are inscribed "JSBach.1733" and contain a host of handwritten corrections and comments. Bach experts have identified the vast majority of these verbal entries as "definitely Bach" or "probably Bach."[4] Hundreds of passages are further scrawled with marginal dashes and other nonverbal markings. Although these are harder to evaluate, physicists at the Crocker Nuclear Laboratory have concluded through ink analysis that "with high probability, Bach was also responsible for the underlinings and marginal marks."[5] Read contextually, this document provides wide-ranging evidence for Bach's premodern Lutheran world- and life view, and it renders absurd the notion that he had progressivist or secularist tendencies.

Bible Reading

Within Calov's printing of Luther's scripture verses, there are many small errors that doubtless would have gone undetected by even the most biblically literate reader. Yet time and again, Bach has restored a text that was far from clearly missing or has changed a perfectly plausible-sounding but unattested wording to the standard Lutheran rendering. Very few of these corrections stem from the list of errors printed in Calov's appendix.[6] Some biblical scholars have concluded from this that Bach may have acted like an astute modern textual critic, poring over Calov's volumes and painstakingly comparing them, line by line, with other Luther Bibles.[7] But there is a simpler and more likely scenario, grounded in conservative eighteenth-century social and devotional practices.

Picture the people of Bach's household on free evenings, gathered in their living room for the activity of reading aloud. The children

[4] Cox, *The Calov Bible*, 3–30.
[5] Cox, *The Calov Bible*, 42.
[6] Calov, *Die heilige Bibel*, VI, unnumbered final 10 pages.
[7] E.g., Cox, *The Calov Bible*, 21.

HANDWRITTEN ENTRIES IN BACH'S BIBLE   33

take turns reciting from a family Bible for practice in reading and elocution, as well as for spiritual edification. The patriarch follows along in his magnificent Study Bible, in part to make sure there is no passage skipping or other tomfoolery from the lectors and in part to allow him to reach for his inkwell whenever he notices an error in Calov's scriptural verses compared with what he has just heard.[8]

Tellingly, in something akin to what linguists call a mondegreen, Bach apparently misconstrued what the children—in this reconstruction of the scene—had said in several passages and emended a scriptural verse's legitimate Lutheran rendering to a similar-sounding but unattested wording. Isaiah 16:8, for example, in Luther's biblical text in Calov, reads: "Denn Hessbon ist ein wüst Feld worden, der Weinstock zu Sibma ist verderbet . . . Ihre Fesser [*sic*; Luther Bibles, 'Feser'] sind zerstreuet, und über das Meer" ("For Heshbon has become a wilderness field; the vine of Sibmah is withered; . . . their [vine branches] are scattered, and over the sea"). Bach had caught sight of Calov's typographical error *Fesser*, but he seems to have slightly misheard a lector's utterance of the correct wording, and he emended Luther's intended *Feser* ("vine branches") to the biblically unattested *Fäßer* ("wine casks"). In Bach's reading, then, a direct translation of the end of this text becomes "Their *wine casks* are scattered, and over the sea."

In 2 Chronicles 35:8, for another example, Bach changed a misspelled but properly attested biblical rendering by Luther to a logical but unattested wording. In Calov, the verse reads, "Seine Fürsten aber gaben zur Hebe freywillig für das Volck, und für die

---

[8] Now and again, however, there are uncorrected errors. For example, as mentioned in Cox, *The Calov Bible*, 24, the words "spricht der Herr" are missing from Calov's printing of Isaiah 54:1 and are not corrected. Given, however, that the verse still makes grammatical sense without that bit of missing text and given that right before this, within the same sentence, the missing biblical text "hatt [*sic*] mehr Kinder" has been handwritten into the margin, this second bit of missing text may have been overlooked simply because a lector was, quite reasonably, not asked to stop reading while the first bit of (logically necessary) missing text was quilled in.

34 CONSTRAINTS OF HISTORY ON INTERPRETATION

Priester und Leviten (nemlich Hilkia, Sacharia, und Jehiel die Füriste [*sic*; Luther Bibles, 'Fürste'] im Hause Gottes unter den Priestern) zum Passah zwei tausend und sechs hundert (Lämmer und Ziegen) dazu drey hundert Rinde." In direct English translation of the proper text, this reads, "But [King Josiah's] princes freewillingly gave as offering for the people, and for the priests and Levites (namely, Hilkiah, Zechariah, and Jehiel, the *princes* among the priests in the House [i.e., the Temple] of God) for Passover 2,600 (lambs and goats), besides 300 cattle." Bach changed Calov's *Füriste* to *Fürnemstē* (i.e., *Fürnemsten*, which in today's German would be *Vornehmsten*).[9] In Bach's reading, the middle of this text becomes "namely, Hilkiah, Zechariah, and Jehiel, the *foremost* among the priests in the House of God."

Bach cannot have emended Calov's text as the result of a "scholarly," visual comparison of various Bibles—such an approach would have quickly brought to light that the word that Calov printed was actually the one that Luther had written, though misspelled. Bach may well have subconsciously retained in his ear a biblically one-off phrase that may have been read aloud earlier in the evening, 2 Chronicles 31:10: "Asaria der Priester, der *fürnemste im Hause Zadock*" ("Azariah the priest, the *foremost [priest], of the house* of Zadok"). Upon visually encountering the strange three-syllable typographical error "Für- / i-ste," Bach may have thought he had heard a familiar three-syllable utterance, "*Für-nem-sten* im Hause," despite the fact that the person reading 35:8 aloud would have rightly delivered "*Für-ste* im Hause."[10]

The nature of Bach's numerous corrections of printing errors in Calov's biblical passages, then, would reflect Bach having been

---

[9] The Calov Bible had printed this adjectival noun at a hyphenated line break, as "Für- / iste," and Bach simply wrote a small stroke (signifying "n") above the "e" in the new line's "iste" and smothered the printed "i" with his handwritten "nem."

[10] It is probably significant, in this context, that the only instance to be found in the Luther Bibles of any forms of the words *fürnemste*, *in*, and *Haus* appearing next to one another was in 2 Chronicles 31:10.

more of a traditionally devotional, communal reader of scripture than a modern scholarly, individual reader.

Vocation

Of greater direct biographical significance, the Calov volumes elsewhere provide insight into Bach's professional and personal concerns as a director of music, indicating that he understood himself less as a modern artist than as a premodern God worshiper who was following his godly vocation. In Calov's preface to the book of Ecclesiastes, Bach wrote "Summa Libri" ("Summation of the Book") and an "NB," both of which the Crocker Laboratory physicists have filed under "definite Bach entries."[11] Bach's highlightings here make for especially poignant reading, as they take note of passages in the Bible's Solomonic literature that speak of finding godly solace in a world hostile to people faithfully pursuing their divine callings. Sundry administrative records show that Bach often fell into trouble over philosophical differences with his employers about the place of music in worship and in education; these highlighted passages resonate strongly with the concerns and frustrations he expressed in these situations in his own life.[12]

It is worth noting that in his many troubles with his superiors, Bach never gave any hint that he ought to be appreciated and recognized for his artistic talents rather than for his official position in the God-given, biblically revealed vocational hierarchy. What Bach persistently argued was that others had improperly assumed the prerogatives that went with his station. (There is

---

[11] Cox, *The Calov Bible*, 69; see also 23.

[12] The relevant documents are conveniently brought together under the title "Der unbequeme Untergebene" ("The Unwieldy Subordinate") in Hans-Joachim Schulze, ed., *Johann Sebastian Bach: Leben und Werk in Dokumenten* (Leipzig: Deutscher Taschenbuch Verlag, 1975), 40–58.

36 CONSTRAINTS OF HISTORY ON INTERPRETATION

no evidence to suggest that this was simply Bach's disingenuous, calculated strategy for arguing with his hidebound, unmusical employers.)[13]

Music

Only a handful of Bach's entries in Calov concern his specific vocation of composing and performing music, and these have received the most extensive—indeed, typically the only—attention from biographers. Leading writers have striven to explain these marginalia as progressive. In truth, all of the notations straightforwardly reflect conservative Lutheran thinking. What they share is a key premodern interpretive approach to scripture known as typology, whereby events and principles in the era of ancient Israel act as "types" or "shadows" for their correlated "antitypes" or "substances" in the era of Christianity (an approach that is biblically sanctioned most notably by Colossians 2:17).

For example, citing one of Bach's annotations on music as key progressivist testimony, John Eliot Gardiner writes (my italics):

> *Bach understood* that the more perfectly a composition is realised, both conceptually and through performance, the more God is *immanent in* the music. "NB," he wrote in the margin of his copy of Abraham Calov's Bible commentary, "Where there is devotional music, God with his grace is always present." This strikes me as a tenet that many of us as musicians automatically hold and aspire to whenever we meet to play music, regardless of *whatever "God"* we happen to believe in.[14]

[13] See, e.g., Arnold, *Bach*, 58–59.
[14] John Eliot Gardiner, *Bach: Music in the Castle of Heaven* (New York: Knopf, 2013), 17.

This may be an appealing modern idea, but no aspect of it could possibly have been part of Bach's understanding. What Bach noted (next to 2 Chronicles 5:13, concerning music in the Jerusalem Temple under King David) was: "NB. Bey einer / andächtigen *Musique* / ist allezeit Gott mit seiner Gnaden- / gegenwart ("NB. At a [rendering of] devotional *Musique*, God is always manifest by means of his Grace-Presence").[15] This could not have meant what Gardiner claims, namely, that God is *immanent in* well-realized music, because Lutherans like Bach would have condemned as a grievous sin of idolatry any notion that the essence or very being of a piece of music is, or turns into, the essence or very being of God.

Nor is Bach's apparently cryptic note even about the conceivable notion of God's just "dwelling in" or "inhabiting" music (i.e., as opposed to God's becoming, as philosophers would say, "ontologically intrinsic" to the music). The language of Bach's note plainly echoes orthodox Lutheran observations about God and music laid out in Johann Gerhard's *Schola Pietatis*, one of the many books of practical theology listed in Bach's estate inventory.[16] Gerhard wrote the following in his chapter on music,[17] with my italics to indicate the precise correspondence:

> As the voice of the lauding of the Lord was heard . . . then the House of the Lord became filled with a mist, which mist was a symbol and manifestation of the special gracious presence

[15] Bach's *Kurrentschrift* is meticulously transcribed in Schulze, *Bach-Dokumente III*, 636. Corrupted renderings of Bach's German appear often, however, in the secondary Bach literature. Some writers, especially, do not take notice of Bach's line-break hyphenation of the word "Gnadengegenwart" and thus misread the letters of "gegenwart" as if here they constituted a separate word (namely, misunderstood as if it were an adjective, modifying "Gott"—such a meaning, however, would have required "gegenwärtig"), rather than reading it as the second half of a theologically significant one-word compound noun. (Also, it should be mentioned that most published facsimiles of this page from Calov are cropped such that one cannot see Bach's hyphen at the line break.)

[16] Leaver, *Bachs theologische Bibliothek*, 165, established that Bach owned the 1622–1623 edition (five octavo volumes).

[17] Johann Gerhard, "Vom Lob und Preis Gottes," in *Schola Pietatis* (Nuremberg, 1622–1623), III:398r–431r.

38 CONSTRAINTS OF HISTORY ON INTERPRETATION

of God. . . . Now just as the Lord *God* dwelled in the Jerusalem Temple *by means of his Grace-Presence* ["Gnadengegenwart"], in like manner will he also still these days dwell in the hearts of those who laud and praise him.[18]

Thus, the idea behind Bach's remark was not progressivist but doctrinal. The Old Testament text that Bach was commenting on presents the "type" or "shadow": at the sound of the priestly music, the "Glory of the LORD" (Luther Bibles, "Herrlichkeit des HERRN") was summoned to inhabit the literal Temple, manifested by means of a visible "mist" ("Nebel") or "cloud" ("Wolke") enclosing God's invisible Grace-Presence. Bach's marginal note indicates his understanding of the "antitype" or "substance": at a rendering of devotional music, God's Grace-Presence is summoned and will always come to inhabit the hearts of people who are praising God (as performers and listeners).

Bach will have understood the hearts/bodies of Christian believers to be a metaphorical "temple of the Holy Spirit." One of the most well-known passages in the New Testament is 1 Corinthians 6:19, which in Calov reads, "Oder wisset ihr nicht, dass euer Leib ein Tempel des H. Geistes ist, der in euch ist" ("Or do you [plural] not know that your body is a temple of the Holy Spirit, who is in you"). Calov's brief commentary here cites Luther's observation that "Gott kommet herunter in unsere Hertzen, ja in unsere Leibe" ("God comes down into our hearts, yes into our bodies"). Bach's marginal comment, then, has nothing to do with God being "in" music. Rather, summoned by the sound of oratorios, church

---

[18] "Als die Stimme vom Lobe des Herrn gehöret wurde . . . da ward das Haus des HERRN erfüllet mit einem Nebel, welcher Nebel ein Symbolum und Anzeigung war der sonderbaren gnedigen Gegenwart Gottes. . . . Wie nun *Gott* der HERR im Tempel zu Jerusalem *mit seiner Gnadengegenwart* gewohnet, also wil er auch noch heutiges Tages wohnen in den Hertzen derer, so ihn loben und preisen." Gerhard, *Schola Pietatis*, III:405r–405v; quoted in Renate Steiger, "'Gnadengegenwart': Johann Sebastian Bachs Pfingstkantate BWV 172 'Erschallet, ihr Lieder, erklinget, ihr Saiten!,'" in *Die Quellen Johann Sebastian Bachs: Bachs Musik im Gottesdienst*, ed. Renate Steiger (Heidelberg: Manutius Verlag, 1998), 45.

cantatas, motets, and the like, God's Grace-Presence comes down into the hearts of Bach's fellow believers. The distinction is important, because Gardiner's suggestion—that Bach understood that the better a work is executed, the more God (or, indeed, whatever "God" twenty-first-century musicians might believe in) is "immanent in" the music—reflects Bach's own world of belief not as much as it anticipates a modern notion of "art as religion." Bach's understanding was clearly grounded in the standard theology of seventeenth-century Lutheranism.[19]

Proof

Next to another significant passage in his Calov Bible, 1 Chronicles 29[28]:21, Bach wrote, "NB. Ein herrlicher Beweiss, dass neben anderen Anstalten des Gottesdienstes, besonders auch die *Musica* von Gottes Geist durch David mit angeordnet worden" ("NB. A glorious proof that, alongside other provisions of the [ancient Jewish and of the eighteenth-century Lutheran] worship service, *Musica* too was especially ordered by God's spirit through [King] David [of ancient Israel]"). Christoph Wolff's magisterial Bach biography identifies the composer's use of *Beweis* here as an approving nod toward the term's centrality in the progressive methodology of scientific empiricism, a methodology that was held already during Bach's lifetime to be applicable also to theological principles; that is, in this newer view, even in religious matters, God has sanctioned a positive role to human reason as an arbiter of truth, whereas in the older view, only God's revelation should and could be relied upon.[20]

---

[19] Gardiner, *Bach*, 15, appears in an additional way to conflate the genesis and the modern reception of Bach's music when he states, "It carries a universal message that can touch anybody. . . . It springs from the depths of the human psyche and not from some topical or local creed."

[20] Wolff, *Johann Sebastian Bach*, 338–339.

40 CONSTRAINTS OF HISTORY ON INTERPRETATION

But the noun *Beweis* was also still frequently used during the eighteenth century in the very same conservative way it was being used in Bach's marginal note: for the "demonstration" of theological principles through study of biblical revelation alone.[21] See, too, for a parallel example, how the text of Bach's *Christmas Oratorio* uses the word *Beweis* in its conventional pre-Enlightenment, non-scientific sense. The text of the recitative movement 32 proclaims that a believer's heart should safeguard the biblical account of the "miracle" ("Wunder") of Christ's birth as a "sure proof" ("sicheren Beweiss") of salvation. Significantly, Bach further highlighted the passage from 1 Chronicles 28 in his Study Bible by entering quote-like marks alongside Calov's commentary, which specifically affirms the more conservative view about theological principles, namely, by saying that "[wir sollen] in Religions Sachen nichts fürnemen und handeln, ohn sein geoffenbartes Wort" ("In matters of religion, we should presume and do nothing without [God's] revealed Word").

What the passage in Chronicles "proves" for Bach, then, is that his eighteenth-century church music is an "antitype" of which the ancient Jerusalem Temple music was a "type." He sees himself not as an individual, modern artist but as a communal, premodern God worshiper who is fulfilling his calling as a church composer within typologically patterned history.

"Vorspiel"

Modern commentators on Bach's annotations are particularly excited about passages that appear to show Bach saying something

---

[21] As is revealed, for example, by doing a search for book titles containing the word *Beweis* or *Beweiss* in the *Das Verzeichnis Deutscher Drucke des 18. Jahrhunderts*, at http://vd18.de. For older such books with *Beweiss* in their title, one can search *VD17-Datenbank: Das Verzeichnis der im deutschen Sprachraum erschienenen Drucke des 17. Jahrhunderts*, at http://vd17.de.

about one of his own compositions. In the margin next to Exodus 15:20, for example, near the end of the story of the Israelites breaking into joyous antiphonal song upon escaping from Pharaoh and his army (by walking on dry land through the parted Red Sea, which then drowned the Israelites' enemies), Bach wrote "NB. Erstes Vorspiel, auf 2 *Chören* zur Ehre Gottes zu *musiciren*." In a groundbreaking essay on Bach in general, Gerhard Herz offered what has now become a standard view of this annotation:

> The word *Vorspiel* (Prelude) seems puzzling in this context unless Bach intended to refer to the first number, piece, or movement of a multisectional antiphonal work. If we were to look for such a composition, the opening movement for two four-part choruses of the eight-part motet *Singet dem Herrn ein neues Lied* [BWV 225] comes readily to mind. . . . Bach's reading of Exodus 15:20–21, and of Calov's subsequent commentary that sparked his own marginal remark, may have been the creative impulse for the composition of the motet.[22]

Herz rendered Bach's annotation as "*Nota bene*. First Prelude, to be performed with—verbatim: 'on'—2 choirs to God's Glory." Others have accepted Herz's linking of Bach's annotation and the composition of the motet, but they give slightly differing translations of Bach's remark. Howard Cox initially rendered it as "NB. First section for two choirs to be performed to the honor of God," but then later on in the same book, it is given as "NB. First prelude for two choirs to be performed to the honor of God."[23] Thomas Rossin put forward the strange reading "NB Festival

---

[22] Gerhard Herz, "Toward a New Image of Bach," in *Essays on J. S. Bach*, by Gerhard Herz (Ann Arbor, MI: UMI Research Press, 1985), 159–161.

[23] Cox, *The Calov Bible*, 18, 404. The former rendering is adopted in Christoph Wolff, ed., *The New Bach Reader: A Life of Johann Sebastian Bach in Letters and Documents* (New York: W. W. Norton, 1998), 161.

42 CONSTRAINTS OF HISTORY ON INTERPRETATION

prelude for 2 choirs to be sung to the glory of God."[24] And Gardiner provided "NB. First prelude, for two choirs to be performed for the glory of God," also noting in this connection that "the 'first prelude' [in *Singet dem Herrn ein neues Lied*, BWV 225; namely, bars 1–75] eventually leads to a fugue for the children of Zion to dance to."[25]

These translations and their linking of Bach's annotation to his composing of the motet are all problematic. First, as has continued to happen with writers on Bach and Calov, they miss the fact that the leading Bach archival documents expert, Hans-Joachim Schulze, pointed out many years ago that Bach's handwriting in the Calov annotation is from the 1740s,[26] meaning that Bach's annotation cannot possibly have stimulated him to compose the motet, for Bach's handwriting in his score of the motet is from the 1720s.[27] (And, as we will see, Bach's remark here in Calov is unlikely to have had anything to do with any particular piece of Bach's at all, whether composed beforehand or afterward.) Second, Rossin's "*Festival* prelude" is presumably a simple misreading of Bach's *Erstes* (first) as *Festes* (festival). But the main problem lies with that word *Vorspiel*. At a recent Bach colloquium, my great friend and colleague Joshua Rifkin wondered, in a Q&A session for another colleague's paper on the Calov Bible annotation and its link to when and why Bach's *Singet dem Herrn* motet might have been composed, whether perhaps Bach's employment of "*Vorspiel*" in Calov referred not to a prelude at all but rather to some sort of "*Beispiel*" (example). I am convinced, from the word's hitherto unnoticed use in the Calov Bible's printed commentary, that Rifkin was on the right track.

---

[24] Thomas Donald Rossin, "The Calov Bible of Johann Sebastian Bach: An Analysis of the Composer's Markings" (PhD diss., University of Minnesota, 1992), 91, 257–258.

[25] Gardiner, *Bach*, 473.

[26] In 1972, Schulze, *Bach-Dokumente III*, 636, dates this "after 1740(?)"; and then a little over a decade later, in 1985, Cox, *The Calov Bible*, 18, reports that in Schulze's consultation with Cox, "Dr. Schulze would date this after 1740."

[27] www.bach-digital.de/receive/BachDigitalSource_source_00000855.

Vorspiel as used here by Bach is a theological term, and Calov's commentary on Exodus 25:9 provides an example of its use and meaning:

> This [verse] is one of the main [scriptural] passages wherein Moses testifies that his [religious] regime [i.e., under the God-revealed "law of Moses"] should come to an end and be not the proper crowning essence but a *Fürbild* ("prefiguration") and *Fürspiel* ("before instance") of the kingdom of Christ [under the God-revealed "gospel of Christ"].[28]

We know that Bach had seen this page, and we may reasonably assume that he noticed its use of the word *Fürspiel*, because at the very next verse, 25:10, there is a correction in Bach's handwriting of a striking error in Calov's printing of Luther's biblical text. Calov's verse 10 speaks of the "chest" ("Laden"; i.e., Ark [of the Covenant]) in the Tabernacle being two and a half cubits in length, a cubit and a half in width, and a cubit and a half "in *length*" ("die Länge"). This is obviously illogical, and Bach duly crossed out "Länge" at the end of Calov's verse and wrote "Höhe" ("height") just below it.

Bach's "Vorspiel," then, is another spelling of Luther's "Fürspiel." (*Für* and *vor* are essentially interchangeable in older German, where it is the surrounding accusative or dative contexts that affect and effect the meanings.) Luther's "Fürspiel" is one of the many German terms for "type" that are employed in his (and Calov's) theological contrasting of type and antitype. "Schatten" ("shadow") and "Fürbild" (or "Vorbild," "prefigurement") have already been mentioned, and other such terms include "Schattenwerck"

---

[28] "Das ist der Haupt-Sprüche einer, darinnen Moses zeugt, dass sein Regiment soll auffhören und nicht das rechte endliche Wesen, sondern ein Fürbild und Fürspiel seyn des Reiches Christi." Calov, *Die heilige Bibel*, I:541; Calov does not mention that this commentary here quotes verbatim what Luther had printed in the margin of his Old Testament translation, next to Exodus 25:9. The word *Fürspiel* is also used elsewhere in Calov; for example, in his commentary on Exodus 2:12.

44 CONSTRAINTS OF HISTORY ON INTERPRETATION

("shadow work") and "Figuren" ("figures"). "Fürspiel" (or "Vorspiel") is a much rarer use, but it is attested. So a historically more informed, if rather clunky, rendering into English of Bach's "NB. Erstes Vorspiel, auf 2 Chören zur Ehre Gottes zu musiciren" would be "NB. [This is the] first 'before instance' [in the Bible] of rendering music with 2 choirs to the honor of God."

What Bach's remark-to-self appears to mean is that he thought it was worth noting that the antiphonal singing of the ancient Israelites in Exodus 15 is the first of the divinely revealed types/ shadows in the Bible that point to Christian antiphonal music as their antitype/substance. In fact, Exodus 15 had been hailed as a quintessential example for typology since earliest Christianity. In 1 Corinthians 10:1–6, the Red Sea event is seen as a "baptism into Moses" that serves as a prefigurement ("tupos" in biblical Greek; "Fürbild" or "Vorbild" in the Luther Bibles) of Christian baptism. Every time Bach beheld the baptismal font in the Thomaskirche in Leipzig, he would have seen, etched into one of its panels, a quotation of Hebrews 11:29, which speaks of the Israelites having gone "by faith" through the Red Sea; and because this is a baptismal font, he and others would have taken for granted the typological connection to the Exodus 15 story that was famously expounded in Corinthians.[29]

Similarly, every time Bach beheld the opened organ casing in the Nikolaikirche in Leipzig, he would have seen a powerful typological construal of the very phenomenon he was noting in his "Vorspiel" annotation. Church records indicate that the case's left panel depicted the Red Sea scene and its attendant antiphonal choir singing from Exodus 15, and the right panel depicted the choir singing—likewise believed to be antiphonal—in Revelation 4.[30]

---

[29] A photograph of this panel is printed in Martin Petzoldt and Joachim Petri, *Bach—Ehre sei dir Gott gesungen: Bilder und Texte zu Bachs Leben als Christ und seinem Wirken für die Kirche* (Berlin: Evangelische Verlagsanstalt Berlin, 1986), 153.

[30] Martin Petzoldt, *Bachstätten: Ein Reiseführer zu Johann Sebastian Bach—Mit zahlreichen Abbildungen* (Frankfurt: Insel Verlag, 2000), 158. One gets a bit of a sense of

So it now seems clear that Bach's annotation about the music-making at the Red Sea was meant to acknowledge a theological connection between the song recorded there and all later Christian antiphonal choir music. Once again, we see evidence of Bach's devout interest and belief in broad patterns of divinely ordered history and not, in this case, a documentational link to his possibly having looked for and found inspiration, like the artists of subsequent eras, in order to create a particular "masterwork" in one's career as a Great Composer.

Leviticus

Some of Bach's annotations have prompted modern scholarly commentary that questions how those markings can have been theologically relevant to him at all. In a recent Bach biographical essay, Robert Marshall—my beloved Doktorvater—wrote (italics mine):

> Can we say that, in [pursuing fugue and canon], Bach was *determined* to *master* the *"law,"* as manifested in music, to *conquer* it and *make it his servant*? We know from the Calov Bible commentary that Bach annotated the book of *Leviticus*, the third book of *Moses*. It is interesting that he *bothered* to read Leviticus *at all* (with its *innumerable* rules and prohibitions pertaining to sacrificial rites, permitted and forbidden foods, *sexual crimes*, slavery, property rights, and so on), *that he knew it so well*, and that he *cared* about these *arcane* and, *for a Christian, irrelevant* laws.[31]

the typological contrast from the watercolor painting of the organ that is reproduced in Michael Maul, *Bach: Eine Bildbiografie* (Leipzig: Lehmstedt, 2022), 223.

[31] Robert L. Marshall, "Young Man Bach: Toward a Twenty-First-Century Bach Biography," in *Bach and Mozart: Essays on the Enigma of Genius*, by Robert L. Marshall (Rochester, NY: University of Rochester Press, 2019), 21. Marshall is heavily influenced in his approach (reflected, as well, in his essay title) by the interpretively interesting but historiographically rather controversial Erik H. Erikson, *Young Man Luther: A Study in Psychoanalysis and History* (New York: W. W. Norton, 1958).

46   CONSTRAINTS OF HISTORY ON INTERPRETATION

But Christians need not have thought the book of Leviticus "arcane" or "irrelevant," and Bach certainly did not require some special psychological motivation to have been interested in it.

The one extensive handwritten verbal entry of Bach's in the book of Leviticus is next to 18:16, which reads, with Calov's commentary in parentheses: "Du solt deines Brudern Weibes ([ausser] wenn derselbe stirbet, oder sich von ihr geschieden) Scham nicht blössen, denn sie ist deines Bruders Scham" ("You shall not bare your brother's wife's pudenda[32] ([except] if that man dies, or has divorced her), for it [the woman's 'Scham'] is your brother's pudenda"). Bach wrote in the margin: "NB. Scheinet dem Gesetze (so da ordnete, dass ein Bruder seinem verstorbenen Bruder Saamen erwecken solt) *contrair* zu seyn" ("NB. Appears to be *contraire* to the Law [of Moses] (regulated there [in Deuteronomy 25:5–10] such that a brother shall [marry his childless sister-in-law and] breed progeny [to be accounted] to [the lineage of] his dead brother").

It nicely happens that there is documentary evidence suggesting that Bach consulted Deuteronomy 25:5–10 in his Calov Bible when he made the unspecified biblical cross reference in his annotation at Leviticus 18:16. Bach's marginal comment clearly borrows some of its wording from a German translation of an excerpt from Luther's *Deuteronomion Mosi cum annotationibus* of 1525 printed in Calov's commentary at Deuteronomy 25:9, which begins: "Herr Lutherus: Das Gesetz des Bruders Frau zu nemen, oder von den Samen, der für dem gestorbenen Bruder sol erweckt werden" ("Herr Luther: The law about taking [i.e., marrying] the wife of the [dead] brother, or about the progeny that shall [thereby] be bred [in order] to [continue the lineage of] the dead brother"). Bach's handwritten

---

[32] Because Luther, in line with Western tradition, calls the female genitalia "Scham" (literally, "shame"), I have used an English equivalent for the translation (that is, I am not endorsing the notion that body parts are shameful!). The *Oxford English Dictionary* gives as the etymology for the word "pudendum": "classical Latin *pudendum*, literally 'that of which one ought to be ashamed,' use[d] as noun (usually in plural, *pudenda*, to denote the external genitals) of neuter gerundive of *pudēre*, to cause shame, ashame."

HANDWRITTEN ENTRIES IN BACH'S BIBLE   47

"verstorbenen" is slightly less brusque in tone than Calov's printed "gestorbenen," but the likelier explanation for Bach's word choice is just that he was being biblically more exacting than the German translator of Luther's Latin commentary had been. *Verstorbene* (not *gestorbene*) is the word for "dead" that was used for Luther's biblical text in Deuteronomy 25.

Cox reports, "It is [Calov's] comment [i.e., "if that man dies," a phrase that ought to have been prefaced by the word "except"], not the text [of Leviticus 18:16], which contradicts the law [in Deuteronomy 25] to which Bach refers."[33] It is difficult, however, to credit Cox's confident notion that at the margin of Leviticus 18:16, Bach was making an observation about Calov's parenthetical comment but not about the biblical text itself. Calov's comment, as printed, is utterly and inescapably contrary to what the law in Deuteronomy says. Whatever Bach is talking about in his marginal note, however, is something that he says "*appears to be* contrary"— that is, Bach's annotation would concern something that might only seem to be conflicting.

The concern of Bach's annotation surely did extend to the biblical text. As Cox, an Old Testament scholar, must or should have known, for centuries, Jews and Christians had, and have, resolved what they saw as an only apparent conflict here by taking the directive in Deuteronomy to be a specific exception to the general rule in Leviticus.

What, then, about Marshall's amazement that Bach cared in the first place about the laws in the book of Leviticus, purportedly irrelevant to a Christian? For the case of Leviticus 18:16, that question is easy to answer, as this law—whatever its jurisprudential status—will without question have been far from irrelevant to a Christian, and Bach certainly need not have had some quasi-Freudian personal reason for being interested in it. This is because the passage in Leviticus and the connected one in Deuteronomy are related to an

---

[33] Cox, *The Calov Bible*, 19.

48 CONSTRAINTS OF HISTORY ON INTERPRETATION

important and well-known New Testament story, in Mark 12:18-27 (with parallels in Matthew 22:23-33 and Luke 20:27-40).

In that story, Jesus is approached by some Sadducees who ridicule him about belief in the resurrection of the dead. Citing the authority of the levirate law, they posit a test case that they reckon ought handily to disprove the idea of resurrection. They ask Jesus what would happen if six brothers in a row married their previous dead brother's ever-childless wife—which of these seven men would the woman be married to in the resurrection? All sorts of historical, theological, and other complications come to bear on an understanding of this biblical narrative, but for present purposes, it suffices to say that Jesus does not respond by declaring the levirate law to be no longer jurisprudentially valid. He says, rather, that there is no marriage at all in the afterlife, and he goes on to quote other material from the Hebrew Bible as support for his teaching on resurrection.

So there is nothing "personal" or mysterious or odd about Bach's interest in Leviticus—the book was theologically relevant to Christian thought, and it was quoted, closely alluded to, or paraphrased often enough in the New Testament.[34] That was surely sufficient reason for Bach, and indeed any biblically minded Christian, to have cared about it and to have found it relevant.

Conclusion

In his article on Bach biography, Marshall rightly observed, "In general, we have hardly begun to learn the lessons that the Calov

---

[34] Most famously, Leviticus 19:18 ("Love your neighbor as yourself") in Matthew 5:43, Matthew 19:19, Matthew 22:39; Mark 12:31–33, Luke 10:27, Romans 13:9, Galatians 5:14, and James 2:8. See also Leviticus 11:44 in 1 Peter 1:16; Leviticus 12:8 in Luke 2:24; Leviticus 16:2 and 16:12 in Hebrews 6:19; Leviticus 16:27 in Hebrews 13:11; Leviticus 18:5 in Romans 10:5 and Galatians 3:12; Leviticus 19:2 in 1 Peter 1:16; Leviticus 19:12 in Matthew 5:33; Leviticus 20:7 in 1 Peter 1:16; Leviticus 24:20 in Matthew 5:38; and Leviticus 26:12 in 2 Corinthians 6:16.

HANDWRITTEN ENTRIES IN BACH'S BIBLE   49

Bible has to teach us about Bach's theological and even existential outlook."[35] I hope the present chapter is to some degree useful in responding to that desideratum.

My suspicion is that many of us long for a great musical figure like Bach to have been a great thinker who conveys immortal thoughts on the human condition that are personal, modern, and individual to him. But as far as I can tell from the historical evidence, Bach's (essentially orthodox Lutheran) world- and life views were suprapersonal, premodern, and not individual to him.[36]

The renowned writers on Bach biography discussed in this chapter have interpreted Bach's Calov annotations as supporting their images of Bach as a quasi-Freudian, identity-crisis-ridden genius; or as a quasi-scientific, learned empiricist scholar; or as a quasi-pantheistic, broadly ecumenical aesthete; or as a Great Artist finding special creative stimuli to compose individual works. With wider and deeper knowledge of relevant historical materials, however, these views look like contextually improbable anachronisms— impositions of a modern mindset on an early-eighteenth-century figure.

The common theme running through the disparate surface subject matter of Bach's extended annotations is Christian typology. Considered in this light, Bach's comments reflect his interest not in sex crimes, in powerful father figures like the musician King David, in scientific reasoning, or in universalist art–religion, but in the

---

[35] Marshall, "Young Man Bach," 21.

[36] For details on how Bach's other annotations in his Calov Bible correlate in general to the concerns reflected and promoted in Bach's extensive repertory of liturgical and secular vocal music, see Marissen, "Bach against Modernity" (reprinted in the present volume as chapter 1). That essay shows how the conservative outlook expressed in Bach's vocal music is continually paralleled in his Calov notations. Most of Bach's vocal music was composed from the 1710s to the 1730s, whereas his Calov notations were entered in the 1730s and 1740s. This situation, however, makes the Calov notations more, not less, biographically significant. In view of the fact that almost all the private notations come not before but well after the public compositions (and thus, the notations cannot be simply written off as Bach's engaging in disinterested research to meet unwelcome liturgical duties, in order to "pay the rent"), we can logically infer that Bach did subscribe to the sentiments expressed in his vocal music.

50 CONSTRAINTS OF HISTORY ON INTERPRETATION

godly order underlying the relationship of the past to the present and future. For many who may have been haunted by the misgiving that history might be "just one damned thing after another," the coherence within the meta-patterns of the revealed truth of biblical typology would have provided tremendous assurance and comfort.

Wolff, the most important by far of today's myriad Bach biographers, has curiously referred to the many sixteenth- and seventeenth-century books listed in Bach's estate as "quasi-shelf-warmers."[37] These sorts of materials may have been passed over by Bach's children as unappealing, but any suggestion that they had held faint interest for Bach himself would have to be nothing but baseless speculation, and any suggestion that these older materials would by and large have been outdated and therefore generally of little or no interest to readers during and after Bach's day would appear likewise to be radically unjustified: nearly every one of these titles listed in Bach's theological library was reprinted in either the eighteenth or the nineteenth century, or both.

Bach's ownership of these volumes and his assenting engagement with their ideas, reflected in the theologically nuanced entries he made in his Bible commentary, point to a life steeped in a pre-Enlightenment Lutheran worldview. It is very difficult to square that with a desire to drag him into the thought worlds of modernity.

---

[37] Wolff, *Johann Sebastian Bach*, 334, where Bach's library, likewise curiously, is called a "scholarly collection of theological literature" (perhaps to tally with Wolff's image of Bach as a "learned" figure?). A scholarly theological library would have been dominated by "folio" (large-format) volumes of learned disquisitions in Latin. Bach's collection, however, consists overwhelmingly of books of practical theology in German, and most of its titles are in "quarto" or "octavo" (small formats), as is typical of more devotional and pastoral materials like these.

PART II
BRIEF COMMENTARIES

3

Fractal Gavottes and the Ephemeral World in Bach's Cantata 64

J. S. Bach—now, there is a composer who knows that gilded tombs do worms enfold. As his parishioners learned already soon into his tenure as music director for the Leipzig churches, he was prepared to see to it that even the most festive liturgical occasions had their relatively grim moments.

Consider *Sehet, welch eine Liebe hat uns der Vater erzeiget*, BWV 64, a Christmas cantata whose soprano aria gives powerful expression to a cheerless view of the world that is encountered often in the poetry from Bach's vocal music. Its text reads (with my emphases, to highlight the biblical allusions):

> What *the world*
> Contains
> Must, *like smoke, fade away.*
> > *But* what Jesus gives me,
> > And what my soul loves,
> > *Remains,* securely and *eternally.*[1]

Even the casual listener can readily hear how this aria's elegant courtly dance rhythms serve to represent "the world" and how its occasional upwardly trailing-off violin and vocal lines evoke wisps of "smoke."

---

[1] "Was *die Welt* / In sich hält, / Muss *als wie ein Rauch vergehen.* / Aber was mir Jesus gibt, / Und was meine Seele liebt, / *Bleibet* fest und *ewig stehen.*"

Bach against Modernity. Michael Marissen, Oxford University Press. © Oxford University Press 2023.
DOI: 10.1093/oso/9780197669495.003.0003

54 BRIEF COMMENTARIES

But Bach's compositional engagement with the aria's poetry is deeper and much more interesting than this.

As background, it is important to know that several verbal conceits are closely based on passages from Martin Luther's translation of the Bible. To begin with, there is 1 John 2:17, "*The world, with its delight, fades away; but* whoever does the will of God, he *remains* into *eternity*."[2] And then there is also Psalm 37:20, "*Like smoke fades away,* the enemies of the Lord will *fade away*."[3] These sentiments from Psalm 37 may, correspondingly, put one in mind of James 4:4, "Whoever wants to be the world's friend, he will be God's enemy."[4]

Our aria from Cantata 64 opens with the orchestra performing a textbook example of a specific dance's phrase structure, which is made up of a two-beat + two-beat "call" (bars 0b–1a + 1b–2a) followed by a four-beat "answer" (bars 2b–4a). This dance is called a "gavotte."

The vocal and instrumental lines of the aria fall in with the melody-and-accompaniment textures of French-style gavottes, as opposed to the more complex textures of Italian-style gavottes. And the smaller pulses of both of the two-beat "call" melodies yield two short-short-long gestures (such that the short is exactly half the length of the long), which is also a highly conventional gavotte formula: namely, ta-ta-DA / ta-ta-DA.

A second phrase (bars 4b–8a) divides in the same way, and here the melody's surface rhythm, strikingly, is a flurry of running sixteenth notes all the way through the phrase. Even so, one can readily sense from the accompaniment that this music proceeds from an underlying ta-ta-DA gavotte gesture directly into the section's closing material.

---

[2] "Die Welt vergeht mit ihrer Lust: wer aber den Willen Gottes tut, der bleibt in Ewigkeit."

[3] "Die Feinde des HERRN . . . werden . . . vergehen, wie der Rauch vergeht."

[4] "Wer der Welt Freund sein will, der wird Gottes Feind sein."

FRACTAL GAVOTTES AND THE EPHEMERAL WORLD   55

What we have, as it happens, within this gavotte section is a virtuoso violin line of the three conventional segments—"statement" (bars 0b–4a), "spinning forth" (bars 4b–6a), and "closing" (bars 6b–8a)—that are frequently found in the ensemble refrains of Vivaldian concertos. Group refrains in baroque concertos are called "ritornellos." So, in Bach's Cantata 64 aria, "the world" of the stately French gavotte "contains" several key elements of the hyperkinetic Italian concerto.

The opening two phrases (bars 0b–4a and 4b–8a), then, constitute the aria's instrumental ritornello. Intriguingly, both of these phrases subdivide into 2 + 2 + 4 beats. That is to say, the beat patterns in this particular phrase structure are, in fact, a quadruple augmentation of the underlying ta-ta-DA rhythm of the conventional gavotte gesture in the aria's very opening melodic snippet. So, in the relative lengths of its internal phrasings, the whole of Bach's ritornello acts as a sort of "super-gavotte."

The way baroque arias work is that some or all of the segments of an instrumental ritornello are performed before and after sections that feature the singer. The singer's sections are called "episodes."

The first vocal episode (bars 8b–24a)—which begins, as many Bach arias do, with the singer melodically quoting the beginning of the instrumental ritornello, in the home key, before migrating to new material—consists of two "super-gavotte" internal phrasings, followed by a third configuration of double this length. That is to say, the respective lengths of the three large subsections in this episode (8 + 8 + 16 beats) are a quadruple augmentation of the already quadruply augmented ta-ta-DA rhythm in the phrasing of the "super-gavotte." Thus, by means of this still-higher-level structure, Bach's first episode acts as a sort of "mega-super-gavotte."

In the second episode (bars 28b–42a), however, these broader gavotte levels fall apart. Though this aspect of the aria's structure is far from obvious in casual listening, it amounts to the initial nail in the coffin for the aria's eventual wide-ranging "fading away" of "the world." Not only the surface puffs of smoke in the virtuoso violin

56 BRIEF COMMENTARIES

line and in the vocal line but also the very framework of the aria's layered gavotte world itself "must fade away."

On top of all but one of the singer's long-note utterances of the words "stehen" and "fest" in the aria's extended middle section (bars 50b–92a), the instruments curiously perform fragments from the aria's ritornello segments in harmonically and melodically distorted versions.

The effect of these passages comes close to surreal. Bach appears, indeed, in this middle section to have put a subtle degree of musical enmity between the singer and the instrumentalists. It is only the singer's own long-held chanted notes that will "remain securely"— each of the Italian concerto elements that "the world" of the French gavotte "contains" will be disfigured or dismembered or both, and their melodic intactness will have "faded away" by the end of this extended section of the aria.

These gavotte and concerto disfigurements and their enmity with the singer's single-pitch chanting in the middle section of the aria do, of course, provide marvelous aesthetic variety, but their creative inspiration may have been just as much biblical as musical: the aria's earlier-mentioned main source text, 1 John 2, specifies that "the world, *with its delight*, fades away"; and furthermore, Psalm 37 clarifies that "the *enemies* of the Lord will fade away." With the "da capo" (the direction to reperform the opening section, bars 1–50, after the cadence in bar 92), the standard organizational patterns and the initial stages of their breakdown, described above, are experienced, then, for a second time.

In conclusion, what might this all mean more generally?

In its public exhorting, our excerpt from Cantata 64 calls attention to several key themes in a premodern Lutheran viewpoint that was continually pitted against what conservative Lutherans like Bach took to be the undue and indeed dangerous optimism of Enlightenment thinking. (By the way, for Bach's private endorsement of the anti-Enlightenment ideas often found in his public vocal works, we can read, for example, his subsequent handwritten annotations, entered mostly during the 1740s, into the margins of his personal study Bible.[5])

Bach's aria forcefully proclaims that:

- The present world is fundamentally not good (it must fade away).
- Humanism and its attainments ultimately add up to nothing (they cannot fundamentally or reliably make the world better; only what Jesus gives will remain).
- Only eternity, not problematic time, is cast-iron (the temporal world, with its ephemeral delights—just like the enemies of the Lord—will fade away).

Bach's aria setting went well beyond any call of duty in underscoring these conservative Lutheran sentiments, and even more generally speaking, what marks his achievement as premodern is the fact that his brilliant artistry gave expression not to rationally or emotionally discovered personal truths but to what were believed to be biblically revealed communal truths.

---

[5] These are explored in Michael Marissen, "The Biographical Significance of Bach's Handwritten Entries in His Calov Bible," *Lutheran Quarterly* 34 (2020): 373–389 (reprinted as chapter 2 in the present volume); and Michael Marissen, "Bach against Modernity," in *Rethinking Bach*, ed. Bettina Varwig (New York: Oxford University Press, 2021), 315–335 (reprinted as chapter 1 in the present volume).

4

Time and Eternities in Bach's Cantata 23

Bach's church cantata *Du wahrer Gott und Davids Sohn* (BWV 23) was one of several pieces he performed on February 7, 1723, in his audition for the job of music director in Leipzig. The work was designed to go with the gospel portion for that Sunday, Luke 18:31–43, a reading that combines a prediction of Jesus's death and resurrection with a story of his healing a blind beggar.

The second movement of the cantata is an extraordinarily expressive recitative for tenor. This recitative acts in part, I suggest, as a nonverbal sonic emblem that evokes several traditional Christian notions of time and eternity in its fostering of spiritual regeneration among Bach's intended audience of premodern listeners.

In order to understand what is going on in Bach's second movement, we need to be familiar with the text of his first movement, a melancholy duet for soprano and alto. Lines 1 and 4 in this duet's poetry are clearly derived from the cantata's attendant gospel portion, where, at Luke 18:38,[1] the beggar cries, "Jesus, you son of [King] David [of Israel], have mercy on me."[2] Line 1 of Bach's duet goes on to significantly expand Luke's messianic acknowledgment—"son of David"—by also hailing Jesus as "true God." Here is the entire text of Bach's duet:

---

[1] This story is also told, with many varying details, in Mark 10:46–52, Matthew 20:29–34, and Matthew 9:27–31.

[2] "Jesu, du Sohn Davids, erbarme dich mein."

Bach against Modernity. Michael Marissen, Oxford University Press. © Oxford University Press 2023.
DOI: 10.1093/oso/9780197669495.003.0004

TIME AND ETERNITIES 59

> [Jesus,] you true God and son of David,
> You who in the distance, from eternity,
> Already closely looked upon my heartache
> And my bodily pain, have mercy on me.
> And through your miracle-working hand,
> Which has averted so much evil,
> Let help/salvation and consolation befall me likewise.[3]

This poetry makes the—for some modern readers, perhaps slightly strange—observation that "in the distance, from eternity, [*Jesus*] *already* closely *looked upon* my heartache." The "distance" here is of both space and time. In classical Christian belief, derived from the Gospel of John, Jesus is the "Logos/Word become flesh." The Logos of God exists outside of temporality and is all-knowing and thus can look closely upon individual humans of all times already before they are born.

Consider, then, the text from Bach's second movement, the ensuing recitative that is the main subject of the present chapter:

> Ah, do not pass by;
> You, the salvation[4] of all humankind,
> Have appeared, yes,
> To minister to the sick and not the healthy.
> Thus I, likewise, partake of your omnipotence;
> I look upon you in these paths
> Where people[5]

---

[3] Translated by Daniel R. Melamed and Michael Marissen. "Du wahrer Gott und Davids Sohn, / Der du von Ewigkeit in der Entfernung schon / Mein Herzeleid und meine Leibespein / Umständlich angesehn, erbarm dich mein! / Und lass durch deine Wunderhand, / Die so viel Böses abgewandt, / Mir gleichfalls Hilf und Trost geschehen!"

[4] "Heilen" means both "to heal" and "to save." Note, too, that upon miraculously granting him sight, Jesus says to the blind beggar in Mark 10:52 and Luke 18:42, "dein Glaube hat dir geholfen" ("your faith/belief has helped/saved you"). See also "Hilf," which means both "help" and "salvation," in line 7 of the first movement of the cantata.

[5] This potentially confusing sentence of lines 6–9, with its reference to "people," is derived from Luke 18:36–39 (and Mark 10:46–48), where many among "the

60 BRIEF COMMENTARIES

> Wished to let me lie,
> Also in blindness.[6]
> I compose myself
> And will not let you go
> Without [receiving] your blessing.[7]

What the tenor essentially proclaims at line 1 is "Ah Jesus, do not pass by without *saving* me." He is quoting from the healing story as told in Luke 18 and Matthew 20, where Jesus was said to be "passing by" on the way to Jerusalem and thus to his crucifixion. Just as the blind beggar wanted to be healed of sightlessness, the "I" of Bach's recitative wants to be "healed"—that is, to be "saved."

What one readily hears in a good performance of Bach's recitative is that there is an otherworldly character to the sound of its instrumental accompaniment.[8] And this accompaniment is especially interesting, in that if the notes of just the top instrumental line are held up to examination, one will see and hear that those are, in fact, pitch-for-pitch, the notes—albeit in very slow motion—of the famous Lutheran hymn "Christe, du Lamm Gottes," whose text reads:

---

crowd"—rendered in the Luther Bibles of Bach's day as "das Volk" ("the people")—sternly commanded the blind beggar to be silent.

[6] The blind beggar of Luke 18 is unnamed, but in Mark 10, he is identified as "Bartimaeus, son of Timaeus." Both gospels describe this man as being "am Wege" ("by [the side of] the path"). The puzzling phrase "sehe . . . auch in der Blindheit an" in Bach's cantata is often translated as "look upon . . . even in [my] blindness," but this does not properly reflect what the story of Bartimaeus entails: it is not that "I" am able to see Jesus "*even* in blindness" but that "I" am able to see Jesus "*also* [i.e., like Bartimaeus] in blindness."

[7] Translated by Melamed and Marissen. "Ach! gehe nicht vorüber; / Du, aller Menschen Heil, / Bist ja erschienen, / Die Kranken und nicht die Gesunden zu bedienen. / Drum nehm ich ebenfalls an deiner Allmacht teil; / Ich sehe dich auf diesen Wegen, / Worauf man / Mich hat wollen legen, / Auch in der Blindheit an. / Ich fasse mich / Und lasse dich / Nicht [gehen] ohne deinen Segen."

[8] I recommend especially the 1998 recording on BIS by Gerd Türk with the Bach Collegium Japan, directed by Masaaki Suzuki, *Bach: Cantatas, Vol. 8* (BWV 22, 23, 75).

TIME AND ETERNITIES   61

Christ, you lamb of God,
You who bear the sin[9] of the world,
Have mercy on us.
Christ, you lamb of God,
You who bear the sin of the world,
Have mercy on us.
Christ, you lamb of God,
You who bear the sin of the world,
Give us your peace. Amen.[10]

Now, an interesting and significant set of circumstances is that when I have played recordings of this excerpt (even for very seasoned Lutheran church musicians), unprompted listeners typically do not comprehend that there is a slow-motion hymn melody here. The first of two kinds of eternity in Bach's recitative is expressed by quoting that hymn in this oblique manner. What the instrumental hymn tune apparently symbolizes is the "singing" of what Luther and Lutherans called the "invisible church," as opposed to what they called the "visible church." The visible church is simply everyone who attends services in ecclesiastical buildings, but the true church is the invisible one that constitutes the "communion of all saints" who are actually "saved" (i.e., from an afterlife in hell).[11] Bach's cantata is all about salvation. So this metaphorical singing of

[9] The phrase "die Sünd" here is singular, not plural: "die Sünd[e]," not "die Sünd[en]." It is derived from John 1:29, which in the Luther Bibles of Bach's day reads, "Siehe, das ist Gottes Lamm, welches der Welt Sünde traget" ("Look, that is God's lamb, which bears the sin of the world").

[10] Translated by Melamed and Marissen. "Christe, du Lamm Gottes, / Der du trägst die Sünd der Welt, / Erbarm dich unser! / Christe, du Lamm Gottes, / Der du trägst die Sünd der Welt, / Erbarm dich unser! / Christe, du Lamm Gottes, / Der du trägst die Sünd der Welt, / Gib uns dein Frieden! Amen." This is the German hymnic version of the Agnus Dei from the Ordinary of the Latin Mass. Bach's composing score of Cantata 23 consisted of only three movements. He later entered another movement, a setting of "Christe, du Lamm Gottes," into the performing parts of the cantata.

[11] Philip Melanchthon, "Apology of the Augsburg Confession," trans. Charles Arand, in *The Book of Concord: The Confessions of the Evangelical Lutheran Church*, edited by Robert Kolb and Timothy J. Wengert (Minneapolis: Fortress, 2000), 174–183.

62   BRIEF COMMENTARIES

the community of saints in Bach's recitative seems to evoke an example of one kind of "eternity," the kind where there is a beginning but no end.[12]

Then, at the end of the recitative, the tenor sings, "I compose myself, and *will not let you go*, [Jesus,] *without [receiving] your blessing*." Those lines are quoting a famous passage from Genesis 32, the foundation story of Israel in which Jacob wrestles with a man or angel—it is a little unclear at first who he is. At the end of the night, that figure says to Jacob, "Let me go." Jacob responds, "I will not let you go unless you bless me." Jacob then realizes that he has seen "God" face to face and, astonishingly, has survived it. Luther was very excited about the idea that the divine figure whom Jacob wrestled with was actually God's Messiah, the divine Son. In his *Lectures on Genesis*, he comments concerning chapter 32: "Without any controversy [!] we shall say that this man [with whom Jacob wrestled] was not an angel but our Lord Jesus Christ, eternal God and future Man, to be crucified by the Jews."[13] In Luther's extreme Christocentrism, then, this man/angel of Genesis 32 was a manifestation of the second person of the Trinity, who had come out of another kind of eternity into time, the kind of eternity that is "timeless" and where there is no beginning or end—an eternity where everything is but one permanent "now," such that, for example, God experiences the past, the present, and the future as if they were simultaneous (following the classic medieval definition of "eternity" as *tota simul* [wholly at once]).

This idea that the second person of the Trinity breaks out of eternity into history well before he becomes manifest as Jesus of Nazareth and dies on the cross also comes up in the Bach motet *Ich*

---

[12] As explained, for example, in the entry on "Ewigkeit" in Christian Stock, *Homiletisches Real-Lexicon oder Reicher Vorrath zur geist- und weltlichen Beredtsamkeit* (Jena, 1734), 398–399.

[13] Martin Luther, *Luther's Works, Vol. 6, Lectures on Genesis: Chapters 31–37*, ed. Jaroslav Pelikan, trans. Paul D. Pahl (St. Louis, MO: Concordia Publishing House, 1970), 144.

lasse dich nicht (BWV 1164), which sets word for word the text of Genesis 32:26. The motet's libretto inserts the words "my Jesus,"[14] to show that it was completely understood that when Jacob said, "I will not let you go unless you bless me," his "you" (unwittingly) referred to Jesus. Luther and his followers are among the only biblical interpreters who thought such a thing, and it is important for understanding the Bach vocal works to know that this is the background.

At the final section of the recitative from Cantata 23, the last note of the instrumental hymn is harmonized inconclusively, such that the hymn's tonal resolution comes from outside. Thus, these various questions that are being asked of God-in-eternity are, in fact, answered musically—not textually—by the rest of Bach's instrumental ensemble declaring V–I (a perfectly resolving cadential ending); that is, by clearly and forcefully declaring a nonverbal "yes." The idea, apparently, is that those various melodic lines from the otherworldly instrumental strands that enter into the world of the recitative are examples of both an "everlasting eternity" and a "timeless eternity" breaking into the present, and it is these eternities that lead to a clear and forceful expression of the positive response that the tenor supplicant is seeking.

The "existential I" of Bach's audition cantata is not a modern individual who achieves ultimate fulfillment through one's own effort, merit, and accomplishment but, rather, a member of an eternal community whom personal salvation "befalls" from outside, through the unmerited gift of divine grace.

Cantata 23 can be heard not simply as an aesthetic manifesto of a modern Great Artist (as is sometimes said about this work) but as a sort of theological-musical manifesto: *this* is what music can do—music can project depths of biblical and theological meaning and experience in ways that words alone cannot.

---

[14] That is, the text of the first movement reads, "Ich lasse dich nicht, du segnest mich denn; / *Mein Jesu*, ich lasse dich nicht, du segnest mich denn!"

5

Bach's *Christmas Oratorio* and a Blessed End

At the bottom of Bach's cover page for the performing parts from Part I of his *Christmas Oratorio*, his son Johann Christoph Friedrich later entered the somewhat curious annotation: "Composed *anno* 1734, in the 50th year of the author."[1]

Turning fifty is a significant milestone for anyone, but Bach may well have felt his coming within reach of this event to be especially unsettling. His father, Johann Ambrosius, had died in 1695 at forty-nine years and 363 days, and his eldest brother, Johann Christoph (his ensuing guardian and tutor), had died in 1721 likewise at forty-nine—both of these powerful figures in Bach's life had passed on "in the 50th year." Moreover, his mother, Elisabeth, had died at fifty.

In December 1734, Bach's fiftieth birthday was just a few months away. Having composed several massive annual cycles of liturgical compositions, he had already effectively achieved what he had once called his "final aim, namely, [the crafting of] a regulated [body of] church music, to the honor of God."[2] But for that year's Christmas obligations, he decided to do something truly special.

Doubtless inspired by his grand-scale biblical works such as the *St. John Passion* and the *St. Matthew Passion*, Bach embarked on the novelty of a six-part *Christmas Oratorio*, featuring a tenor soloist

---

[1] "Componirt anno 1734 / im 50ten Jahre des Verf[assers]."

[2] "Den Endzweck, nemlich eine *regulirte* kirchen *music* zu Gottes Ehren." This appears within Bach's request in 1708 for dismissal from his post in Mühlhausen; printed in Werner Neumann and Hans-Joachim Schulze, eds., *Bach-Dokumente I* (Kassel: Bärenreiter, 1963), 19.

Bach against Modernity. Michael Marissen, Oxford University Press. © Oxford University Press 2023.
DOI: 10.1093/oso/9780197669495.003.0005

BACH'S *CHRISTMAS ORATORIO* AND A BLESSED END   65

chanting the scriptural narratives of the birth of Jesus in recitatives, with interspersed meditations on the story elements appearing in the form of elaborate arias (newly written poems, for various soloists or choir with orchestra) and modest chorales (hymn stanzas, for the choir).

Modern concertgoers generally give their greatest attention to the arias and choruses, being apt to lend a laxer ear to the choir's hymn stanzas and often to pay negligible regard to the tenor's biblical recitation. For Bach, though, at least the visual ranking of the oratorio's verbal content went the other way around: He saw to it that libretto booklets were published for his audiences to peruse, having the chanted biblical texts typeset in a strikingly large Gothic bold, with justified margins, but positioning the choir's hymn texts in smaller Gothic bold, with left and right indentation, and the soloists' arias in small Gothic regular, likewise indented. Both visually and sonically, then, Bach aimed to starkly distinguish the oratorio's biblical narrative from its contemplative commentary.[3]

The extraordinary varieties of musical style and emotion in the commentary sections of Bach's *Christmas Oratorio* can be readily enjoyed for their sheer sound alone. Much of the libretto itself, however, may make little or no sense to modern listeners. Ecstatic expressions of verbal and musical joy at the birth of Jesus the savior, are, of course, altogether straightforward to grasp. What seems harder to work out for audiences today are the oratorio's more sensual passages, with their strange talk of "Zion" and a "bridegroom," or its extensive ruminating on whether the believer's "heart" will be a suitable "dwelling place" for the "bridegroom." To many listeners, more puzzling yet will be the militaristic choruses and arias, including their ultimate claim that with the coming of the baby Jesus, "death, devil, sin, and hell are completely diminished."[4]

---

[3] "Commentary" is used here in a colloquial sense (offering meditations on), not in the academic sense (offering scholarly annotations on the text of a literary work).

[4] Lines 5–6 from the closing chorus: "Tod, Teufel, Sünd und Hölle sind ganz und gar geschwächt."

66 BRIEF COMMENTARIES

Crucial to a proper appreciation of the narrative and commentary in the *Christmas Oratorio* is knowing that Bach's Lutheran contemporaries held to a belief in an interconnected "*threefold coming of Christ*."[5] The First Coming referred to the past, the lowly birth of Jesus "in a harsh manger." The Second Coming referred to the present, the dwelling of Jesus in the hearts of his followers—indeed, a *literal* indwelling in the case of the sacrament of communion, where Jesus was said to be physically present "in, with, and among"[6] the elements of bread and wine. And finally, the Third Coming referred to the future, the End Time, when Jesus would return in glory to judge the living and the dead, to destroy once and for all the powers of evil, and also to be the "bridegroom" at a great apocalyptic feast, spoken of at Revelation 19:7, which would celebrate the "marriage" of Christ, "the Lamb of God," to his Zion, the Church—"the bride," who "makes herself ready," an idea touched on already at the very first aria in the *Christmas Oratorio*.

The text chosen for the final movement of the oratorio came, atypically, from a hymn that was little known to Bach's original audiences. The tune he employed for these words, however, was extremely well known. Many of today's concertgoers will, because of its prominent use in Bach's *St. Matthew Passion*, be put in mind of the *Passion* hymn "O Sacred Head Now Wounded,"[7] but in Bach's day, the far more likely textual association for this melody was the funeral hymn "Herzlich tut mich verlangen" ("With my Heart[8] Do I Long for a Blessed End").

What the expression "a blessed end" indicated was "to depart from this life into the glory of a blessed afterlife in heaven."

---

[5] For full background, see Markus Rathey, *Johann Sebastian Bach's* Christmas Oratorio: *Music, Theology, Culture* (New York: Oxford University Press, 2016), 52–64.

[6] "In, mit und unter."

[7] "O Haupt voll Blut und Wunden" (literally, "O Head Full of Blood and Wounds").

[8] *Herzlich* usually means "sincerely" or "heartily," but here it is used in the sense of "with my heart" (i.e., what I feel, inwardly), as typically opposed to *mündlich* ("with my mouth"; i.e., what I say, outwardly).

That is to say, as Bach pondered personal (and communal) death, he was surely not longing for posthumous fame and glory as a modern, autonomous Great Artist.

Writing in his fiftieth year what he may truly have imagined would be his swan song, Bach would have had particularly good cause to be pondering time and eternity. Thankfully, he lived for another fifteen years, though, bringing forth further spectacular compositions such as the *Art of Fugue* and—his actual opus ultimum—the *Mass in B minor*.

6

Bach and Art and Mammon

I was honored to have been asked, in the summer of 2020, to write the following brief observations as a foreword to, and endorsement of, Noelle Heber's marvelous book on Bach and material and spiritual riches.[1]

*

Before the troubled times of the current Covid-19 pandemic which became a worldwide crisis earlier this year, my music history students would typically find remote and quaint, and even a bit humorous, such sentiments as are expressed in Bach's Cantata 102:

> Heut lebst du, heut bekehre dich!
> Eh morgen kömmt, kanns ändern sich;
> Wer heut ist frisch, gesund und rot,
> Ist morgen krank, ja wohl gar tot.

> Today you are living; convert [to godliness] today!
> Before tomorrow comes, things can change;
> One who today is vigorous, healthy, and ruddy,
> Is tomorrow sick—sure enough, quite dead.

At present, however, the concerns of Bach's day are seeming rather less foreign.

In Bach's world, blood infection was a continual threat, a mere scratch on the knee could easily in no time leave you "quite dead,"

---

[1] Noelle M. Heber, *J. S. Bach's Material and Spiritual Treasures: A Theological Perspective* (Woodbridge, UK: Boydell, 2021).

Bach against Modernity. Michael Marissen, Oxford University Press. © Oxford University Press 2023.
DOI: 10.1093/oso/9780197669495.003.0006

BACH AND ART AND MAMMON 69

and disease was rampant. Today we have antibiotics, but for how long will they still work? And we have vaccines for many diseases, but will we have one anytime soon for this terrifying Covid-19?[2] In Bach's world, even the well-off could not really afford to be cavalier about food and money. Today the same has rapidly become true again for even the well-off.

By the same token, in Bach's world, the arts appear to have been valued more for spiritual comfort and enjoyment than for the modern, more centrally driving forces of entertainment, amusement, and "pure" aesthetic contemplation. His contemporaries certainly would rarely, if ever, have appreciated art as something that was in any way worthier than material necessities such as food and shelter. The wording of Sirach 41:11 in their Luther Bibles (which is 40:22 in other Bibles) nicely and forcefully summed matters up: "Dein Auge sihet gern, was lieblich und schön ist; aber eine grüne Saat lieber denn die beide" ("Your eye likes to see what is lovely and beautiful, but a green crop more than the both of them"). Today, especially during this pandemic, people are increasingly realizing that "art for art's sake"—with its advocating a near-total separation from the material concerns of life—is a romantic notion whose sell-by date has long passed.

J. S. Bach's Material and Spiritual Treasures, then, is an extraordinarily welcome and timely book for scholars and other enthusiasts who seek in their appreciation of Bach to be better informed about the concrete historical realities of early-eighteenth-century life and music. With unusual skill and sensitivity, its author has marvelously succeeded in being detailed and painstaking but not dry, in being biblical and theological but not religiose, and in being sophisticated and of-the-moment but not faddish.

---

[2] Update, two years later: In the meantime, we indeed have vaccines for COVID-19 and many people seem to have already forgotten just how terrifying life was in the summer of 2020.

Bach emerges more clearly and persuasively than ever as a real flesh-and-blood human being who was glad to honor God and to enjoy (but not serve) mammon and not just, or even primarily, to have labored for artistic and other recognition.

Thank you, Noelle Heber!

PART III
TEXTS

PART III

7

Historically Informed Renderings
of the Librettos from Bach's Cantatas

With coauthor Daniel R. Melamed

Neither historically informed writing on Bach nor historically informed performance has given enough attention to an essential question: what did the decidedly premodern German texts that Bach set in his church cantatas and secular cantatas most likely mean to their creators and listeners? More careful and thorough historical work in religion, Bible, culture, and language can provide well-grounded answers.[1] We, as coauthors, have now embarked on the project of devising direct translations, with annotations, for all of Bach's cantatas,[2] and we offer excerpts from our ongoing findings here in seven categories: (1) problems of meaning in singing translations, (2) problems of rendering verbatim biblical passages, (3) problems of misconstruals involving archaic language, (4) problems of full or partial misconstruals involving Lutheran biblical language, (5) problems of unwarranted modern editorial emendation of German text, (6) problems of modern editorial mistranscribing of German text from Bach's untidy

[1] This chapter overlaps in approach and conclusions, but not in repertorial and other content, with Michael Marissen, "Historically Informed Rendering of the Librettos from Bach's Church Cantatas," in *Music and Theology: Essays in Honor of Robin A. Leaver on His Sixty-Fifth Birthday*, ed. Daniel Zager (Lanham, MD: Scarecrow, 2007), 103–120; reprinted as chapter 2 of Michael Marissen, *Bach & God* (New York: Oxford University Press, 2016).

[2] These materials are being posted, for free use, at Michael Marissen and Daniel R. Melamed, Texts and Historically-Informed Translations for the Music of Johann Sebastian Bach, http://bachcantatatexts.org.

Bach against Modernity. Michael Marissen, Oxford University Press. © Oxford University Press 2023.
DOI: 10.1093/oso/9780197669495.003.0007

74 TEXTS

handwriting, and (7) problems of spotty or missing punctuation in the original Bach sources. Each of these problems has led to less than satisfactory—or even misleading—understandings of the texts of Bach's music.

Singing Translations

Many published translations of the librettos from Bach's cantatas are designed to accommodate non-German-language performances of the works, focusing on matching syllable counts, preserving word order, providing rhymes, and aligning syllables with musical rhythms, particularly in arias and chorales. For these and other reasons, such translations often substantially alter the meanings of the German librettos.

Consider, for example, the text of the closing movement from Bach's well-known church cantata *Himmelskönig, sei willkommen*, BWV 182:

> So lasset uns gehen in Salem der Freuden,
> Begleitet den König in Lieben und Leiden,
> Er gehet voran
> Und öffnet die Bahn.

Charles Sanford Terry, a leading Bach scholar of the early twentieth century, offers the following rendering in English:

> Then let us go onward to Salem with singing,
> Our hearts and our sorrows before His path flinging!
> He goeth before,
> Mankind to restore.[3]

---

[3] Charles Sanford Terry, *Joh. Seb. Bach: Cantata Texts, Sacred and Secular; with a Reconstruction of the Leipzig Liturgy of His Period* (London: Constable, 1926), 203.

Terry's rendering in English is remarkably skillful in maintaining the scansion and rhyme scheme of its German source text, and performing Bach's cantata with Terry's text may well help modern choirs of English speakers who do not know German "feel" more closely what it might be like to perform Bach with full verbal awareness of what they are singing. But Terry's text is only loosely useful for understanding what Bach's librettist actually wrote.

The sense of Cantata 182's original German poetry is even more distant in the rendering of Henry Drinker, a noted Bach enthusiast, whose singing translations have been widely used, including even in program notes provided for cantata performances in German:

> So let us then hasten to Salem rejoicing
> To be with our Master forever and ever,
> Our Saviour and Guide,
> Whatever betide.[4]

Terry's translation exhorts listeners on their heavenly journey to *fling their sorrows away*, but the German source text, in a theologically much more nuanced and partly opposing directive, exhorts listeners on their heavenly journey to *share in the sorrows* of God's Messiah. Drinker's translation exhorts listeners *to hurry* (*on their way*) to heaven *to be* with God's Messiah (readily conveying the sense that *they have decided* to follow him), but the original (purely and simply) urges them *to go* with God's Messiah, who *opens the way for them* (conveying the sense that *God's Messiah has decided to make it possible for them* to follow him).

Here, then, is our direct translation of the German:

---

[4] Henry S. Drinker, *Texts of the Choral Works of Johann Sebastian Bach in English Translation* (New York: Association of American Colleges, Arts Program, 1942–1943), 345.

76   TEXTS

So let us go into the Jerusalem[5] of joy,[6]
Accompany the king in love and suffering;
He goes on ahead
And opens up the pathway [for us into heaven].

Rendering Verbatim Biblical Passages

Another problem in understanding the librettos from Bach's cantatas is that many translations simply copy their biblical excerpts verbatim from standard English Bibles such as the King James Version, the New Revised Standard Version, or the New International Version. These Bibles often reflect neither the readings of the particular Hebrew and Greek sources for Luther's German Bible nor the specific language Luther used in rendering them in German nor the premodern Lutheran interpretive understanding of his particular translations, all of which contribute to the background for the texts that Bach set to music.

Cantata translators are especially likely to use the King James Bible, as its language is familiar and aesthetically beautiful, and its text is in the public domain. Differences of meaning between the German texts from the Luther Bibles of Bach's day and their corresponding passages in the King James Bible, however, can be significant and far-reaching.

Take, for example, Bach's church cantata *Es ist nichts Gesundes an meinem Leibe* (BWV 25), whose opening movement is a setting of Psalm 38:3 as rendered in the Luther Bibles of Bach's day:

---

[5] "Salem" is the locality where Melchizedek was king, according to Genesis 14:18. Salem is traditionally identified with Jerusalem, in part because of the parallelism between "Zion" and "Salem" in Psalm 76:2. Hebrews 5:10 says that Jesus was designated by God to be a (sacrifice-administering) high priest in the order of Melchizedek.

[6] Here the "n" in "Freuden" is probably an old-fashioned singular genitive ending, not plural. The "Jerusalem of joy" is the "heavenly Jerusalem" of Hebrews 12:22.

HISTORICALLY INFORMED RENDERING OF LIBRETTOS   77

Es ist nichts Gesundes an meinem Leibe vor deinem Dräuen und ist kein Friede in meinen Gebeinen vor meiner Sünde.

Richard Stokes, in his book of cantata translations,[7] copies the rendering of the King James Bible, capitalizing, however, the first letter of "thine," here a pronoun for God:[8]

There is no soundness in my flesh *because of* Thine *anger*; neither is there any *rest* in my bones *because of* my sin.

Here is our direct rendering of the German of the Luther Bibles of Bach's day, as it appears in Cantata 25's libretto:

There is nothing healthy in my body *in the face of* your [i.e., of God's] *threatening*, and no *peace* in my bones *in the face of* my sin.

Some of the differences of meaning here between the English and German Bibles are subtle. The expression underlying Luther's

---

[7] Richard Stokes, *Johann Sebastian Bach: The Complete Church and Secular Cantatas* (Ebrington, UK: Long Barn, 1999), 40.

[8] This practice of editorially capitalizing pronouns, if applied without proper attention, can lead to strongly inaccurate interpretation. Stokes, *Johann Sebastian Bach*, 268, via King James wording but with several editorially capitalized pronouns, renders the text of the second movement from Bach's church cantata *Erschallet, ihr Lieder* (BWV 172), a verbatim setting of John 14:23 in the Luther Bibles of Bach's day, as "If a man love me [Jesus], he will keep my words: and [God] my Father will love him, and we [*Jesus and his followers*] will come unto Him [*my Father*], and make our abode with Him [*in heaven*]." But this is the reverse of what the biblical text (and the rest of Cantata 172) proclaims. In Luther's German, John 14:23 reads, "Wer mich liebet, der wird mein Wort halten, und mein Vater wird ihn lieben, und wir werden zu ihm kommen und Wohnung bei ihm machen." In our direct translation, we render this as "Whoever loves me [Jesus], he will keep my word, and [God] my father will love him; and we [*God the father and Jesus*] will come to him [*the man who keeps my word*] and make [*our*] dwelling place [*on earth*] in [*the body of*] him [*the man who keeps my word*]." According to New Testament teaching, God inhabits the Christian believer's body as a "temple." For example, in the Luther Bibles of Bach's day, 1 Corinthians 6:19 reads, "Wisset ihr nicht, dass euer Leib ein Tempel des Heiligen Geistes ist, der in euch ist, welchen ihr habt von Gott, und seid nicht euer selbst" ("Do you [followers of Jesus] not know that your body is a temple of the Holy Spirit, who is in you, whom you have from God, and you are not your own"). In Cantata 172, there are many allusions to this teaching.

78 TEXTS

"in the face of" that is employed in the original Hebrew text of the psalm can mean "because of" or "in the face of," and most interpreters of Psalm 38's usage go with the former, while Luther opted for the latter. And the Luther Bible's "Friede" ("peace") is closer to the widely familiar underlying Hebrew noun ("shalom") than the King James's "rest."[9] But the difference in meaning between the English Bible's "anger" and the German Bible's "Dräuen" is profound. "Dräuen" is an older German spelling of "Drohen" ("threatening"). The noun employed in the original Hebrew text of Psalm 38 means God's "rage" or "indignation," but in Luther's idiosyncratic translation, a wilder, more inscrutable, and thus more starkly premodern God is depicted as *threatening* the sinner.

Reflecting the Luther Bible's distinctive reading of the psalm, Bach's musical setting is extremely foreboding and melancholy— the music is not "angry," the mood that Stokes's rendering would lead one to expect.

An even more striking example of the problems of distorted meaning that stem from a translator's reliance on the King James Bible is provided by Bach's church cantata *Herr, deine Augen sehen nach dem Glauben* (BWV 102), whose opening movement is a setting of Jeremiah 5:3 from the text of the Luther Bibles in Bach's day:

> Herr, deine Augen sehen nach dem Glauben. Du schlägest sie, aber sie fühlens nicht; du plagest sie, aber sie bessern sich nicht. Sie haben ein härter Angesicht denn ein Fels und wollen sich nicht bekehren.

Stokes copies the rendering of the King James Bible (capitalizing, however, the pronouns for God and substituting an exclamation mark for a question mark at the end of the first sentence):[10]

---

[9] Regarding the word "rest," historical King James Bibles here note, however, in the margin, "Heb[rew]. peace, or health."

[10] Stokes, *Johann Sebastian Bach*, 166.

HISTORICALLY INFORMED RENDERING OF LIBRETTOS 79

Lord, are not Thine eyes upon *the truth*! Thou hast stricken them [the people of Israel], but they have not grieved; Thou hast consumed them, but they have refused to receive correction; they have made their faces harder than a rock; they have refused to *return* [to *the truth*].

Here is our direct rendering of the German. An important matter to note is that these things (said of the people of Israel) are expressed not in the present-perfect or past tense but in the "historical present" tense (also known as the "dramatic present" or "narrative present" tense), a creative situation that allows this passage, recalling a past event, to be read simultaneously as a present occurrence:

Lord, your eyes look for *faith*. You strike them [the people of Israel], but they do not feel it; you torment them, but they do not mend their ways. They have a face harder than a rock, and do not want to *convert* [to *faith* in you].

Luther's distinctive and extremely tendentious rendering of Jeremiah 5:3 taps more forcefully into a key premodern interpretive approach to scripture known as "typology," whereby events and principles in the era of ancient Israel act as "types" or "shadows" for their correlated "antitypes" or "substances" in the era of Christianity (an approach that is biblically sanctioned most notably by Colossians 2:17).

The central word here is "Glauben," Luther's word for faith/belief in God. The underlying Hebrew expression in Jeremiah 5:3 is "emunah," signifying not (a commitment to) "faith/belief" but (a commitment to) "firmness," "steadfastness/integrity," "fidelity/truth." Luther's rendering of "emunah" as "Glauben" chimes with his rendering of the New Testament sentiment in Hebrews 11:6, "ohne Glauben ists unmöglich, Gott zu gefallen" ("without faith/belief it is impossible to please God"). What is

80 TEXTS

taken to be the "type" of proper faith/belief in the God of Israel is understood to anticipate the "antitype" of the proper faith/belief in God that includes faith/belief in Jesus as God's Messiah and divine Son. In other words, hearing the word "faith" in the passage from Jeremiah would have been theologically significant to Lutheran listeners in a way that translating it as "truth" does not capture.

The other highly significant typological word choice in this passage is "bekehren" ("to convert"). The underlying Hebrew expression here, "shub," means not "to convert" but "to return" or "to turn back." Luther's choice to translate this as "convert" (in the religious sense) makes for a stronger foreshadowing of the prickly issue of Jewish unbelief in Jesus, that is, of Jewish disinclination to *convert* to Christianity. Bach's cantata was written for the Tenth Sunday after Trinity, an occasion on which his fellow Lutheran congregants, counted as members of God's "new Israel," were sternly warned about the sins of "old Israel" (the non-Christian Jews of the first century CE who did not accept Jesus as God's Messiah or divine Son, and later Jews) and about how "old Israel" was punished through God banishing its people after he destroys the Jerusalem Temple. The general message of sermons and cantatas for that day, including Bach's, was that sinful Lutherans could expect similar punishment if they remained unrepentant in their straying from proper Christian belief and behavior.[11] This is clearly how a Lutheran listener in Bach's time would have understood the words of the cantata, in particular the word "bekehren," and a translation seeking to convey early-eighteenth-century understanding ought to reflect that.

---

[11] For a detailed discussion of the background to these materials, see Michael Marissen, "The Character and Sources of the Anti-Judaism in Bach's Cantata 46," *Harvard Theological Review* 96 (2003): 63–99; reprinted as chapter 3 of Marissen, *Bach & God.*

Misconstruals Involving Archaic Language

Another problem with many translations is their reliance on modern German usage and meanings. Word forms, senses, and spellings were often different in Bach's time, and one has to approach his cantata texts with an eye to early-eighteenth-century meanings. We have aimed to do that in our work, relying on contemporary dictionaries,[12] modern historical dictionaries,[13] and scholarly works that examine the older German of Bach's cantatas.[14]

A particularly instructive example is found in the alto aria from Bach's church cantata *Himmelskönig, sei willkommen* (BWV 182), whose complete text reads:

> Leget euch dem Heiland unter,
> Herzen, die ihr christlich seid!
> Tragt ein unbeflecktes Kleid
> Eures Glaubens ihm entgegen,
> Leib und Leben und Vermögen
> Sei dem König itzt geweiht.

[12] Christian Ludwig, *Teutsch-Englisches Lexicon, worinnen nicht allein die Wörter samt den Nenn- Bey- und Sprich-Wörtern, sondern auch so wol die eigentliche als verblümte Redens-arten verzeichnet sind* (Leipzig, 1716).

[13] Johann Christoph Adelung, *Grammatisch-Kritisches Wörterbuch der Hochdeutschen Mundart (Ausgabe letzter Hand, Leipzig 1793–1801)*, digitized version in Wörterbuchnetz des Trier Center for Digital Humanities, Version 01/21, https://www.woerterbuchnetz.de/Adelung; Jacob Grimm and Wilhelm Grimm, *Deutsches Wörterbuch von Jacob Grimm und Wilhelm Grimm*, digitized version in Wörterbuchnetz des Trier Center for Digital Humanities, Version 01/21, https://www.woerterbuchnetz.de/DWB; Jacob Grimm and Wilhelm Grimm, *Deutsches Wörterbuch von Jacob Grimm und Wilhelm Grimm / Neubearbeitung (A–F)*, digitized version in Wörterbuchnetz des Trier Center for Digital Humanities, Version 01/21, https://www.woerterbuchnetz.de/DWB2; Karl Friedrich Wilhelm Wander, *Deutsches Sprichwörter-Lexicon von Karl Friedrich Wilhelm Wander*, digitized version in Wörterbuchnetz des Trier Center for Digital Humanities, Version 01/21, https://www.woerterbuchnetz.de/Wander.

[14] Lucia Haselböck, *Bach Textlexikon: Ein Wörterbuch der religiösen Sprachbilder im Vokalwerk von Johann Sebastian Bach* (Kassel: Bärenreiter, 2004); William B. Fischer, *When God Sang German: Etymological Essays about the Language of Bach's Sacred Music* (independently published, 2017).

82 TEXTS

This aria often receives overly somber performances nowadays, in part because of contextual misunderstanding of what the words "leget unter" mean here and in part because of grammatical and lexical misunderstanding of what the expression "tragt ein unbeflecktes Kleid ihm entgegen" signifies.

Here are the main published English translations of this aria text, with passages at issue marked in italics:

UNGER[15]

Lay yourselves (before) the Savior *(down)*,
{*Prostrate yourselves before* the Savior,}
Hearts, that Christian are!
{All ye hearts that are Christian!}
   Bring (the) unspotted garment
   Of-your faith *to-meet-him*,
   (Let) body and life and possessions
   Be to-the king now consecrated.
   {Be now consecrated to the King.}

STOKES[16]

Prostrate yourselves before the Saviour,
Hearts of all Christians!
   Clothe yourselves in a spotless robe
   Of your faith, *and go out to meet Him*,
   May your body, your life and possessions
   Be dedicated now to the King.

---

[15] Melvin P. Unger, *Handbook to Bach's Sacred Cantata Texts* (Lanham, MD: Scarecrow, 1996), 634. Note that Unger's translations are word by word, retaining the German text's word order as well. Thus, where English requires two words to render one German word from the source text, Unger will link the English words with dashes (e.g., "Eures" becomes "Of-your," not "Of your"); where the German text implies an extra word in English or where the German text requires a nonliteral rendering to make sense in English, Unger will place the English words in brackets; and where the resulting line of English words is misleading or significantly awkward, Unger will provide within curly brackets a second rendering (e.g., "Lay yourselves (before) the Savior (down)" is given a second time as "{Prostrate yourselves before the Savior}").

[16] Stokes, *Johann Sebastian Bach*, 284.

HISTORICALLY INFORMED RENDERING OF LIBRETTOS   83

JONES[17]

Lay yourselves down before the Saviour,
O hearts that are Christian!
  Wear an unblemished garment
  Of your Faith *to meet Him*;
  May your life and limb and possessions
  Now be consecrated to the King.

AMBROSE[18]

Lie before your Savior *prostrate*,
Hearts of all who Christian are!
Don ye, too, a spotless robe
  Of your faith in which *to meet him*;
  Life and body and possessions
  To the king now consecrate.

DELLAL[19]

Lay yourselves beneath the Savior,
hearts that are Christian!
  Wear the spotless garment
  of your faith *before him*,
  your body, your life, and your *desires*
  should now be consecrated to the King.

One of the keys to understanding the text of this aria is knowing that its first line is playing with language from the story in Matthew 21:1–9 that is traditionally called "The Triumphal Entry [of Jesus into Jerusalem]." In the Luther Bibles of Bach's day, verses 7–8 read: "[Die

---

[17] Alfred Dürr, *The Cantatas of J. S. Bach: With Their Librettos in German-English Parallel Text,* translated and revised by Richard D. P. Jones (Oxford: Oxford University Press, 2005), 258.

[18] Z. Philip Ambrose, *J. S. Bach: The Vocal Texts in English Translation with Commentary: Third Revised Edition* (Bloomington, IN: Xlibris, 2020), 450.

[19] Pamela Dellal, "Bach Notes and Translations," https://www.emmanuelmusic.org/bach-translations/bwv-182.

84 TEXTS

Jünger] brachten die Eselin, und das Füllen, und *legten ihre Kleider* darauf, und satzten ihn darauf; aber viel Volks breitete die Kleider auf den Weg" ("The disciples [of Jesus] brought the donkey, and the colt, and *laid their garments* on them, and sat him [Jesus] on them [the donkey and the colt]; but many of the people spread their garments [as before a king] upon the path [over which Jesus was riding into Jerusalem]"). The opening line of the aria would have been understood in light of this language, and a translation needs to reflect it: "*Lay yourselves* [*as* '*garments*'] *beneath* the savior."

The other key to understanding the text of this aria begins with sorting out the grammar properly in lines 3–4. It is not the case, as Melvin P. Unger, Richard Stokes, Richard D. P. Jones, and Z. Philip Ambrose have inferred, that there are two verbs here. These four translators take their first verb to be (the accusative-taking) "tragen," and they thus render the sense of the command "*Tragt* ein unbeflecktes Kleid" either as "*Bring* a spotless garment" or "*Wear* a spotless garment." They then take the word "entgegen" to be a clipped form of the (in this instance, dative-taking) verb "entgegenkommen," tied to the (dative-receiving) pronoun "ihm." That is to say, they read the lines such that the sense of the whole of their poetically unclipped command would have read, "*Tragt* ein unbeflecktes Kleid eures Glaubens ihm *entgegenzukommen*," thus yielding the sense of the cantata's command as "*Bring/ Wear* a spotless garment of your faith *to meet* [*up with*] him [the Savior]"). Pamela Dellal infers instead that the lines feature one verb, "tragen," along with the (in this instance, dative-taking) preposition "entgegen," yielding the sense of the cantata's command as "*Wear* [a] spotless garment of your faith *before* him."

Neither of these approaches appears to be correct. Rather, what we suggest is going on here is that lines 3–4 employ only the single (in this instance, accusative-taking) separable verb "entgegentragen," which is an archaic synonym for the separable verb "antragen" ("to offer up"). That is, the indirect object (dative) of the verb "entgegentragen" in "*Tragt* ein unbeflecktes Kleid

HISTORICALLY INFORMED RENDERING OF LIBRETTOS 85

entgegen" is the pronoun "ihm." Thus, a word-by-word rendering would be:

Tragt [-]	ein	unbeflecktes	Kleid	eures	Glaubens	ihm	[-] entgegen.
Offer	a	spotless	garment	of your	faith	to him	up.

In a somewhat convoluted metaphor, then, the pure hearts of Christian faith are being likened in the cantata to the literal garments in Matthew 21:1–9 that were *offered up* to Jesus and placed so that they, the garments, would *lie beneath* him.

Our rendering of the aria reads:

> Lay yourselves [as "garments"] beneath the savior [Jesus],
> You hearts that are Christian.
>> Offer up a spotless garment
>> Of your faith to him;
>> Let body and life and means[20]
>> Now be consecrated to the king.

A second example involving unrecognized archaic language is found in Bach's extremely well-known church cantata *Wachet auf, ruft uns die Stimme* (BWV 140), the last lines of whose fifth movement read:

> Vergiss, o Seele, nun
> Die Angst, den Schmerz,
> Den du erdulden müssen;

---

[20] The word "Vermögen," in the present context, could be singular or plural, and its sense could have to do with human "abilities" or material "possessions," or both. It is rendered here as "means" because this solution seems to cover both senses and because this English word, plural in form but singular or plural in construction, works as a translation of the singular "[das] Vermögen" as well as of the plural "[die] Vermögen." It is possible, though unlikely, that the word "Leben" in this line of poetry is likewise plural; and it is possible, though rather unlikely, that "Leib" is to be read as the plural "Leiber" with the "er" syllable poetically clipped off. Note, however, that the German expression "Leib und Leben" corresponds to the English expression "life and limb."

86 TEXTS

Auf meiner Linken sollst du ruhn,
Und meine Rechte soll dich küssen.

Here are the main published English translations of this recitative text, with wordings at issue marked in italics:

UNGER[21]

Forget, O soul, now
The fear, the pain,
Which thou *to-suffer hast-had*;
{Which thou *hast had to suffer*;}
Upon my left-hand shalt thou rest,
And my right-hand shall thee *kiss*.
{And my right hand shall *embrace* thee.}

STOKES[22]

Forget now, O soul,
The fear and grief
You *have had to bear*;
On my left hand shall you rest,
And my right hand shall *embrace* you.

JONES[23]

Forget now, O soul,
The fear, the pain
That you *have had to endure*;
Upon my left hand you shall rest,
And my right hand shall *kiss* you.

AMBROSE[24]

Forget, O soul, forget

---

[21] Unger, *Handbook*, 488.
[22] Stokes, *Johann Sebastian Bach*, 225.
[23] Dürr, *The Cantatas*, trans. Jones, 649.
[24] Ambrose, *J. S. Bach*, 358.

HISTORICALLY INFORMED RENDERING OF LIBRETTOS   87

The fear, the pain
Which thou *hast had to suffer*;
Upon my left hand shalt thou rest,
And this my right hand shall *embrace* thee.

DELLAL[25]
Forget, O soul, now
the fear, the pain
which you *have had to suffer*;
upon my left hand you shall rest,
and my right hand shall *kiss* you.

In this example, all except Jones and Dellal are apparently hesitant to render the cantata's seemingly strange "meine Rechte soll dich *küssen*" as "my right [*hand*] shall *kiss* you." Hesitancy appears to be warranted, as the cantata line is clearly adapted from Song of Songs 8:3 (also 2:6), which in the Luther Bibles of Bach's day reads, "und seine Rechte *herzt* mich" ("and his [the Beloved's] right [hand] *embraces* me"). A ready and appealing solution is just to go with the sense of the biblical word, "embraces." But a better, historically more informed solution lies in realizing that the cantata's verb "küssen"—which is not biblical in origin and which is used here because it rhymes with the poetry's verb "müssen"—is apparently meant to convey not the word's common sense of "to kiss" but its older sense of "to *cushion*."[26] As a result, both clauses in the cantata's couplet promise rest and repose rather than affection or embracing.

We offer the following translation as more likely capturing the sense of the cantata poetry:

[I, Jesus, say to you:]
Forget now, o [Christian] Soul [to whom I am betrothed],

---

[25] Dellal, "Bach Notes and Translations," https://www.emmanuelmusic.org/bach-translations/bwv-140.

[26] In older German, the noun "Kissen" ("pillow," "cushion") was spelled "Küssen."

88 TEXTS

The fear, the agony
That you *have to endure*;
Upon my left [hand] shall you rest [your head],[27]
And my right [hand] shall *cushion* you.

Full or Partial Misconstruals Involving Lutheran Biblical Language

Before delving into specific examples of unrecognized or misunderstood biblical language in the Bach cantatas, it is worth noting and emphasizing that the wordings in today's "Luther Bibles" differ substantially from those of Bach's day[28] and that it is thus crucial to consult historical Bibles such as the versions (with commentary) edited by Abraham Calov and Johann Olearius known to have been in Bach's personal library.[29] (Seventeenth- and eighteenth-century Luther Bibles are close to the wordings of the 1545 Luther Bible but update its orthography.)[30] Our translations rely on the word choices of Luther's text as it was known in Bach's time.

It is also worth noting that there are modern reference works that attempt to indicate places where Bach's cantatas quote or allude to Luther's translation of the Bible.[31] Recognizing these passages is

---

[27] In Song of Songs 8:3 (also 2:6), the Luther Bibles of Bach's day read, "seine Linke *liegt unter meinem Haupt*, und seine Rechte herzt mich" ("his left [hand] *lies under my head*, and his right [hand] embraces me").

[28] Especially troublesome is the heavily revised text of 1984, published by the German Bible Society as *Die Bibel: Nach Martin Luthers Übersetzung, Neu Bearbeitet* (*The Bible: after Luther's Translation, Newly Revised*), which is often referred to, confusingly and misleadingly, as "the Luther Bible"—its bindings typically advertise its contents as *Die Bibel: Lutherübersetzung* (*The Bible: Luther Translation*); the same problem, naturally, holds true for the further revised text of 2017.

[29] Calov, *Die heilige Bibel*; Johann Olearius, *Biblische Erklärung: Darinnen, nechst dem allgemeinen Haupt-Schlüssel der gantzen heiligen Schrifft*, 5 vols. (Leipzig, 1678–1681).

[30] The fantastically convenient searchable Bible presented as "Luther Bibel 1545 (LUTH1545)" at the website https://www.biblegateway.com is not, in fact, the unaltered text of the 1545 Luther Bible. Its wordings are, however, much closer to the texts of the Bibles from Bach's day than modern so-called Luther Bibles are.

[31] Ulrich Meyer, *Biblical Quotation and Allusion in the Cantata Libretti of Johann Sebastian Bach* (Lanham, MD: Scarecrow, 1997); Petzoldt, *Bach-Kommentar*.

HISTORICALLY INFORMED RENDERING OF LIBRETTOS   89

essential to grasping how a religious text might have been heard and understood in Bach's time. But these modern works are problematic as well, sometimes suggesting vague or loose associations between cantata poetry and scriptural texts even when particular and specific references are probably intended. In our translations, we have tried to better identify allusions and references wherever they clearly affect understanding of the libretto, and we have also tried to fully provide, in Luther's German and its direct English translation, the scriptural passages that the poetry refers to.

We do not list biblical quotations or allusions, no matter how close or striking they are, if they do not alter understanding of the libretto or affect the wording of its translation. In Bach's time, one of the purposes of the cantatas and their language was to recall biblical passages and cast light on their meanings; we moderns are in the position of using the Bible, specifically the German Luther Bibles of Bach's day, to shed light on the Bach cantatas, a paradoxical inversion of interpretation.

The opening chorus from Bach's well-known church cantata *Jesu, der du meine Seele* (BWV 78) provides an especially good example of the historically informed interpretive value of recognizing and accommodating significant biblical language.

> Jesu, der du meine Seele
> Hast durch deinen bittern Tod
> Aus des Teufels finstern Höhle
> Und der schweren Seelennot[32]
> Kräftiglich herausgerissen,
> Und mich solches lassen wissen
> Durch dein angenehmes Wort,
> Sei doch itzt, o Gott, mein Hort!

---

[32] Not "Seelennot" ("anguish of the soul") but "Sündennot" ("anguish of sin") in the original hymn and in the printed text booklets that were made available to Bach's fellow congregants at the 1724 performance of this cantata in Leipzig.

90 TEXTS

Here are the main published English translations of the cantata's use of this hymn text, with the word at issue marked in italics:

UNGER[33]
Jesus, who thou my soul
{Jesus, thou who my soul}
Hast through thy bitter death
Out-of the devil's dark cavern
and - oppressive affliction-of-soul
Forcefully torn-out (to freedom)
And me (this) let know
{And hast assured me of this}
Through thy *pleasant* Word,
Be indeed now, O God, my refuge!

STOKES[34]
Jesus, who has wrested my soul
Through Thy bitter death
From the devil's dark cavern
And from oppressive anguish
Most forcefully
And hast informed me of this
Through Thy *pleasant* Word,
Be even now, O God, my refuge!

JONES[35]
Jesus, by whom my soul,
Through Your bitter Death,
From the devil's dark cave
And heavy affliction of the soul,
Has been forcibly torn out,
And You have let me know this

---

[33] Unger, *Handbook*, 273.
[34] Stokes, *Johann Sebastian Bach*, 129.
[35] Dürr, *The Cantatas*, trans. Jones, 523.

HISTORICALLY INFORMED RENDERING OF LIBRETTOS 91

Through Your *agreeable* Word,
Be even now, O God, my refuge!

AMBROSE[36]
Jesus, thou who this my spirit
Hast through thy most bitter death
From the devil's murky cavern
And that grief which plagues the soul
Forcefully snatched forth to freedom
And of this hast well assured me
Through thy *most endearing* word,
Be e'en now, O God, my shield!

DELLAL[37]
Jesus, You, who my soul,
through your bitter death,
out of the devil's dark pit
and the heavy anguish of the soul
have powerfully rescued,
and have let all this be known to me
through your *delightful* Word,
be now, O God, my treasure!

In the theological world of Cantata 78's libretto, it does not quite sound right to translate Jesus's "angenehmes Wort" in the stanza's next-to-last line as his "pleasant," "agreeable," "most endearing," or "delightful" word (or Word). The adjective "angenehm" in common discourse typically does indeed mean "pleasant," "comfortable," and the like. But the sense in Cantata 78 probably echoes Luther's usage of "angenehm" for his rendering of a key New Testament statement, in 2 Corinthians 6:2, "Sehet, jetzt ist die *angenehme* Zeit; jetzt ist der Tag des Heils!" ("Look, now [with the arrival of God's Messiah, Jesus, who

---

[36] Ambrose, *J. S. Bach*, 208.
[37] Dellal, "Bach Notes and Translations," https://www.emmanuelmusic.org/bach-translations/bwv-78.

92 TEXTS

is 'the Word,' according to John 1:14] is the *acceptable*[38]/*favorable*/*propitious*[39] time; now is the day of salvation").[40] Luther described the expression "angenehme Zeit" as a Hebraism, employed in Hebrew scripture to typologically refer to God's "Evangelische Zeit" ("time of the gospel"), a propitious time marked by forgiveness and mercy in Jesus. Thus, the Luther Bibles of Bach's day, for example, render Psalm 69:14 as "Ich aber bete, HERR, zu dir zur *angenehmen* Zeit" ("But I pray, LORD, to you at the *acceptable/favorable/propitious* time").[41]

So the following translation more likely captures the proper sense of the cantata's hymn poetry, with "propitious Word" capturing the contemporary Lutheran understanding of Jesus's word as a source of salvation:

> Jesus, you who through
> Your bitter death have,
> With strength, torn my soul
> From the devil's dark cave
> And from the heavy anguish of the soul,
> And have made me to know this
> Through your *propitious* Word,
> Be even now, O God, my refuge.

A discomfiting example of easily misunderstood cantata poetry that derives its proper sense from biblical language is the A section from the third movement of Bach's extremely well-known church cantata *Ich will den Kreuzstab gerne tragen* (BWV 56):

> Endlich, endlich wird mein Joch
> Wieder von mir weichen müssen.

---

[38] That is, "acceptable" in its sense of "capable or worthy of acceptance"—not in its other sense, of "tolerable or allowable."

[39] From the classical Latin "propitius," meaning "favorably inclined."

[40] This verse appears verbatim in Bach's Cantata 147.

[41] The first two lines of the aria that is movement 34 in Bach's *St. Mark Passion* (BWV 247), "Angenehmes Mordgeschrei! Jesus soll am Kreuze sterben," should probably be rendered in English as "*Propitious* [i.e., as opposed to '*pleasant*'] shout of murder [i.e., the shouting of 'crucify him']; Jesus shall die on the cross."

HISTORICALLY INFORMED RENDERING OF LIBRETTOS   93

Here are the main published English translations of this aria text, with the wording at issue marked in italics:

UNGER[42]
Finally, finally, *must my yoke*
Again from me *be lifted.*

STOKES[43]
At last, at last *my yoke*
Shall fall from me again.

JONES[44]
Finally, finally, *my yoke*
Must be removed from me again.

AMBROSE[45]
One day, one day *shall my yoke*
Once again *be lifted* from me.

DELLAL[46]
Finally, finally *my yoke*
must fall away from me.

The subtle grammatical and lexical challenges in understanding and translating this couplet begin with the question of how to accommodate the German text's use of the piled-up verb "weichen müssen werden" with the noun "Joch" as its subject.

In the absence of being linked with "Joch," no one would readily read "weichen" in the sense of either "to lift," "to fall," or "to remove"—the conventional meanings of "weichen" are "to soak

---

[42] Unger, *Handbook*, 188.
[43] Stokes, *Johann Sebastian Bach*, 93.
[44] Dürr, *The Cantatas*, trans. Jones, 581.
[45] Ambrose, *J. S. Bach*, 143.
[46] Dellal, "Bach Notes and Translations," https://www.emmanuelmusic.org/bach-translations/bwv-56.

94 TEXTS

[something]," "to budge," "to lose ground," "to yield [to something]," or "to give way [to something]." The conspicuous German-biblical language of these lines in Cantata 56 suggests, however, that here "weichen" is meant to be understood in the sense of "to give way." "Weichen müssen werden" in the sense of "to give way," specifically with "Joch" as its subject, is the very language that the Luther Bibles employed in expressing the belief that the law of Moses is to be superseded by the gospel of Jesus. The wording of our cantata couplet and its apparently intended meaning stems from the highly idiosyncratic rendering of Isaiah 10:26–27 in the Luther Bibles of Bach's day and its Lutheran interpretation:

> Alsdenn wird der HERR Zebaoth . . . seinen Stab, den er am Meer brauchte, aufheben wie in Egypten; zu der Zeit *wird* seine Last *von* deiner Schulter *weichen müssen*, und sein *Joch von* deinem Halse, denn das *Joch* wird verfaulen für der Fette.
>
> Thereupon [i.e., on that future day] the LORD Sabaoth will . . . lift up, as in Egypt, his staff which he [the LORD] used at the [Red] Sea [in Exodus 14]; at that time his burden *will have to give way from* your shoulder, and his *yoke from* your neck, for the *yoke* will rot in the face of the [oil from the] fat.

Regarding this puzzling "fat," the gloss in Bach's Calov Bible reads, "von wegen des Oeles damit Christus gesalbet ist" ("[the yoke will rot] because of the oil with which Christ is anointed"); that is to say, the burden of old Israel's Law of Moses *will have to give way* to the liberation of the gospel of Jesus, God's Messiah. The Lutheran understanding Calov reports would, in turn, be reinforced by Acts 15:10, which in the Luther Bibles of Bach's day reads:

> Was versuchet ihr denn nun GOTT mit auflegen des Jochs auf der Jünger Hälse, welches weder unsere Väter noch wir haben mügen tragen?

HISTORICALLY INFORMED RENDERING OF LIBRETTOS 95

Now why then do you [apostles] tempt God with laying of the yoke [of the Law of Moses] upon the neck of the [Gentile] disciples [of Jesus], which neither our fathers [old Israel] nor we have been able to bear?

Thus, Cantata 56's aria is not saying merely that at death, people are freed from the burdens of earthly life. By dint of its idiosyncratic biblical language, the aria is also saying that at death, the burden of the Judaic law will once again have to give way to the freedom the Christian gospel.

We offer the following translation as more likely capturing the sense of the cantata's aria couplet:

Finally [when I die], finally *my yoke* [*of the law*]
Will once again have to give way from me [*in favor of the gospel*].

As a third example of easily misunderstood cantata poetry that derives its proper sense from biblical language, consider the second movement of Bach's extremely well-known church cantata *Ein feste Burg ist unser Gott* (BWV 80.3):

Alles, was von Gott geboren,
Ist zum Siegen auserkoren.
Wer bei Christi Blutpanier
In der Taufe Treu geschworen,
Siegt im Geiste für und für.

Here are the main published English translations of this aria text, with the wording at issue marked in italics:

UNGER[47]
All, that of God is-born,

---

[47] Unger, *Handbook*, 281.

96 TEXTS

Is for victory chosen.
{Has been chosen for victory.}
Whoever (to) Christ's banner-of-blood
In - baptism loyalty has-sworn
{Whoever has sworn loyalty to Christ's banner of
 blood in baptism,}
[Unger has the German source text as "siegt *in
 Christo* für und für"]
Conquers in Christ forever and ever.

STOKES[48]

Every creature born of God
Is destined for victory.
He who at baptism swore loyalty
On Christ's bleeding banner,
His spirit conquers evermore.

JONES[49]

Whatsoever is born of God
Is elected for victory.
Whoever to Christ's Blood-standard
Has in baptism sworn fidelity
Is victorious in spirit for ever and ever.

AMBROSE[50]

All that which of God is fathered
Is for victory intended.
Who by Christ's own bloodstained flag
In baptism swore allegiance
Wins in spirit ever more.

---

[48] Stokes, *Johann Sebastian Bach*, 132.
[49] Dürr, *The Cantatas*, trans. Jones, 707.
[50] Ambrose, *J. S. Bach*, 213.

HISTORICALLY INFORMED RENDERING OF LIBRETTOS   97

> DELLAL[51]
> Everything that is born of God
> is destined for victory.
> Whoever is, with the bloody banner of Christ,
> sworn into the fealty of baptism,
> *conquers in the spirit* again and again.

Unger's rendering speaks of the baptized person triumphing "in Christ." His translation, "conquers *in Christ* forever and ever," correctly corresponds to the German source text that he provides here, "siegt *in Christo* für und für," but this is the wording of a different libretto, the one for Bach's lost church cantata *Alles, was von Gott geboren*, BWV 80.1 (formerly BWV 80a). That lost cantata's wording is derived from 2 Corinthians 2:14, "Aber Gott sei gedankt, der uns allezeit Sieg gibt in Christo" ("But thanks be to God, who at all times gives us triumph in Christ"). The reading in BWV 80.3 is different: "siegt *im Geiste* für und für." As it happens, though, Unger's rendering of the wording from BWV 80.1 is on the right track, even for BWV 80.3.

On the other hand, Stokes's rendering speaks of the triumphing of the baptized person's spirit, Jones's of the triumph of spirit that the baptized person experiences, and Ambrose's of the triumphing in spirit of the baptized person. These are subtle differences, each of these three translations having wrestled in its own way with the apparent ambiguity of the cantata aria's wording. Dellal's rendering, "conquers *in the spirit*," has the significant virtue of being grammatically correct, but it, too, is lexically problematic. All of our translators' renderings, except Unger's, have at least a bit of the modern patina of the "triumphing of the human spirit" to them.

Even though Unger's German-source wording is not the right one, his rendering comes the closest to the most probable sense of Cantata 80.3's line. Evidently, Cantata 80.3's "im Geiste" (i.e.,

---

[51] Dellal, "Bach Notes and Translations," https://www.emmanuelmusic.org/bach-translations/bwv-80.

98   TEXTS

"i[n *de*]*m* Geiste") means not "in *spirit*" but "in [*God*] *the* [*Holy*]
Spirit." In Mark 3:7–8, as given in the Luther Bibles of Bach's day,
John the Baptist declares, "Es kommt einer nach mir, der ist stärker
denn ich; . . . Ich taufe euch mit Wasser, aber er wird euch mit *dem
H. Geist* taufen" ("After me, there will come one who is mightier than
I; . . . I baptize you [believers] with water, but he [Jesus Christ] will
baptize you [not simply with water but also] with *the Holy Spirit*"). If
in the poetry of Cantata 80.1 the baptized person triumphs in God
the Son (the second person of the Trinity), in the poetry of Cantata
80.3 this person triumphs in God the Holy Spirit (the third person
of the Trinity), with the Gospel of Mark's sense of "strength" and
"mightiness" reflected in the battle imagery of the rest of the aria.[52]

We offer the following translation as more likely capturing the
sense of Cantata 80.3's aria:

> Everything born of God
> Is chosen for triumph.
> Whoever in baptism has sworn fealty
> By Christ's banner of blood,[53]
> *Triumphs in the* [*Holy*] *Spirit* ever and ever.

Unwarranted Modern Editorial Emendation
of German Text

Occasionally, the wording in a Bach cantata libretto strikes modern
editors as not making sense, and so they emend the German text.

---

[52] The last line of the third movement in Cantata 80.3 speaks of the "Christi Geist,"
which is sometimes understood today as the "[human] spirit of Christ." The cantata's
expression "Christi Geist," however, was understood in Bach's Lutheranism to refer to
the Holy Spirit and thus should be rendered in English as "the Spirit of Christ." This line
is an allusion to Romans 8:9, which in the Luther Bibles of Bach's day reads, "Ihr aber
seid nicht fleischlich, sondern geistlich, so anders Gottes Geist in euch wohnt; wer aber
Christus [i.e., 'Christi'] Geist nicht hat, der ist nicht sein" ("You [believers in Christ],
however, are not fleshly-minded, but spiritually-minded, if it be that the Spirit of God
dwells in you; but whoever does not have the Spirit of Christ, he [that person] is not his
[God's/Christ's]"). Both the "Spirit of Christ" and the "Spirit of God" were traditionally
understood to be the "Holy Spirit," the third person of the Trinity.

[53] Christ's "banner of blood" is the cross.

HISTORICALLY INFORMED RENDERING OF LIBRETTOS   99

The most well-known example of this occurs in the A section of the duet "Mein Freund ist mein" from Bach's church cantata *Wachet auf, ruft uns die Stimme* (BWV 140), the text of which, in Bach's original performing parts (his score is lost), reads:

> *[Sopran:]* Mein Freund ist mein,
> *[Bass:]* Und ich bin sein,
> *[S & B:]* Die Liebe soll nichts scheiden.

A hyperliteral translation of this would be:

> *[Soprano:]* My friend is mine,
> *[Bass:]* And I am his;
> *[S & B:]* The love shall nothing separate (or,
> Nothing shall separate the love).

Many editions of this cantata emend the reading "*sein*" ("his") here to "*dein*" ("yours"), which on the surface would appear to make much greater sense of the way the dialogue is set out for soprano and bass in the cantata.

"Mein Freund ist mein, und ich bin sein" ("My beloved is mine, and I am his") is the exact wording of Song of Songs 2:16 (and 6:3), where the narrative's female lover voices both of these declarations. Bach's cantata, however, divides the wording of her declarations between its biblical-poetry-borrowing lovers, such that now the word "his" is no longer expressed by the voice of the female to refer to the male lover's possession of her but rather by the voice of the male lover to refer—incoherently, it may seem—to an unspecified male's possession of him. (She: "My friend is mine." He: "And I am somebody else's.")

The male lover in the Song of Songs was traditionally understood in Christian typological interpretation to foreshadow Jesus and the female to foreshadow the Christian soul, whom Jesus would meta-phorically marry at the end time. It thus appears that Bach has here placed the Christian soul's words into the mouth of Jesus but did not change the word "his" to "yours," as we might have expected him to do. The solution to this puzzle becomes clear only from a

100 TEXTS

proper understanding of the next line of the cantata, a line that in our day is continually misread on account of modern unfamiliarity with its origins in idiosyncratic wording from the Luther Bibles of Bach's day.

Before going into those specifics concerning line 3, let us survey how our five main translators have rendered lines 1–3 of the duet:

UNGER[54]

Soprano: My friend is mine,

Bass: And I am his,

Both: (This) love shall nothing sever.

{Nothing shall sever this love.}

STOKES[55]

Soul: My friend is mine,

Jesus: And I am his!

Both: Nothing shall divide this love.

JONES[56]

Soprano: My Beloved is mine,

Bass: And I am his,

Both: Nothing shall separate our Love.

AMBROSE[57]

Soul: My friend is mine,

Jesus: And I am thine,

Both: Let love bring no division.

DELLAL[58]

Soul: My Friend is mine,

---

[54] Unger, *Handbook*, 489.
[55] Stokes, *Johann Sebastian Bach*, 225.
[56] Dürr, *The Cantatas*, trans. Jones, 649–650.
[57] Ambrose, *J. S. Bach*, 358.
[58] Dellal, "Bach Notes and Translations," https://www.emmanuelmusic.org/bach-translations/bwv-140.

HISTORICALLY INFORMED RENDERING OF LIBRETTOS 101

> *Jesus:* and I am yours,
> *Both:* love will never part us [updated from: "Nothing shall divide our love"].

The phrase "Die Liebe soll nichts scheiden" stems from Romans 8:35–39, as rendered in the Luther Bibles of Bach's day, "Wer will uns scheiden von der Liebe Gottes? . . . [Nichts] mag uns scheiden von der Liebe Gottes" ("Who will separate us from the love of God? . . . [Nothing] may separate us from the love of God").[59] The word "nothing" is thus the subject of the duet's third line, and "*the* love"—not "*this/our* love"—is its object. That is to say, the full sense of the German line in Cantata 140's duet appears to be "Nichts soll die Liebe [Gottes von uns] scheiden" ("Nothing shall separate the love [of God from us]").

Bach's duet speaks not of the constancy of Jesus and the soul's love for each other but of the constancy of God's love for the betrothed pair. It thus makes sense that the soul would say "my beloved is mine," that Jesus would say "and I am his [i.e., God's]," and that both would say together "nothing shall separate the love [of God from us]."

We offer the following translation as more likely capturing the proper sense of the cantata poetry, with no emendation of Bach's text needed:

> *Soul:* My beloved is mine,
> *Jesus:* And I am his [—God the Father's];
> *S & J:* Nothing shall separate the love [of God from us].

Modern Editorial Mistranscribing of German Text from Bach's Untidy Handwriting

A striking—and, for some, amusing—example of unlikely textual transcription in a libretto that Bach set to music is found in

---

[59] Note that nearly all Bibles at verse 35 read not "love of God" (i.e., Luther's rendering) but "love of *Christ*."

102 TEXTS

movement 8 of the funeral ode *Lass, Fürstin, lass noch einen Strahl* (BWV 198).

Some modern editions of Bach's cantata and several modern editions of its libretto give the improbable reading "Der Ewigkeit saphirnes Haus . . . tilgt der Erden Dreckbild aus" ("Eternity's sapphiric house . . . blots out the feculent image of earth"). It is true that this reading would chime with such expressions, current in Bach's day, as "Je mehr man den Dreck rühret, je mehr er stinkt" ("The more you stir a turd, the worse it will stink"). But the word printed in the libretto booklets that were distributed at the performance in 1727, replicated in a 1728 book of odes, was not "*Dreck*bild" but "*Denck*bild" (an older spelling of "Denkbild" ["rememorative image"]); and Bach's composing score (his performing parts are now lost), though difficult to decipher, would seem much more likely to indicate "Denckbild" than "Dreckbild."

This is the portion of text, then, that Bach set to music as the A section of his aria:

> Der Ewigkeit saphirnes Haus
> Zieht, Fürstin, deine heitern Blicke[60]
> Von unsrer Niedrigkeit zurücke[61]
> Und tilgt der Erden Denkbild aus.

Of our five main libretto translators, only Jones did not render the text according to the "Dreckbild" reading (but note that Dellal has now rightly updated her earlier rendering):

> JONES[62]
> Eternity's sapphire house

---

[60] In the printed text booklets distributed at the performance in 1727 and in the collection of odes published in 1728, this reads, "Zieht deiner heitern Augen Blicke" ("Draws the serene glances of your eyes").

[61] Text booklet and 1728 book: "Von der verschmähten Welt zurücke" ("Away from the despised world").

[62] Dürr, *The Cantatas*, trans. Jones, 864.

HISTORICALLY INFORMED RENDERING OF LIBRETTOS 103

Draws, Princess, your serene glances
Away from our lowliness
And effaces the *mental image* of the earth.

Each of Jones's colleagues apparently aimed to tone down, to varying degrees, any scatological implications in the misread word "Dreck":

UNGER[63]
Eternity's sapphire house
Draws, (O) Princess, thy (serene) glances
Away-from our low-estate
And blots-out (this) earth's *miry-image*.

STOKES[64]
The sapphire house of eternity,
O Princess, draws back from our humble state
Your cheerful glances
And obliterates earth's *base form*.

AMBROSE[65]
Eternity's sapphiric house,
O Princess, these thy cheerful glances
From our own low estate are taking
And blot out earth's *corrupted form*.

DELLAL[66]
The sapphire house of eternity

---

[63] Unger, *Handbook*, 696.
[64] Stokes, *Johann Sebastian Bach*, 309.
[65] Ambrose, *J. S. Bach*, 506.
[66] Dellal, "Bach Notes and Translations," https://www.emmanuelmusic.org/bach-translations/bwv-198.

104   TEXTS

> draws, O Princess, your fervent gaze
> away from our lowliness
> and removes the remembrance [updated from: "*coarse image*"] of the earth.

We offer the following translation of the apposite German source text—this rendering offers the chance, at least, that we can understand the poet Gottsched's words here—along with a few contextual comments:

> Eternity's sapphiric house
> Draws, Princess, your serene glances
> Away from our lowliness
> And obliterates the *rememorative image* of earth.

"Eternity's sapphiric house" is a poetic reference to the eternal city of Jerusalem (the place where the New Testament says Christians will dwell, resurrected, after the end time), some of whose wall foundations, according to Revelation 21:19, will be emblazoned with sapphire.

The "Princess" is Christiane Eberhardine, wife of August the Strong (elector of Saxony and king of Poland, mentioned in line 5 of movement 2) and honoree of this work. "Fürstin" ("Princess") is short, here, for "Kurfürstin" ("Electress"). The designation "Queen" appears in movements 7 and 10; this is a title Christiane Eberhardine disdained, and its presence in the ode was probably intended to please her husband, who was very much invested in the titles of King and Queen. In movement 7, she is spoken of as a "Glaubenspflegerin" ("preserver of faith"), as she was much admired by her Saxon subjects for remaining staunchly Lutheran after her husband's conversion to Roman Catholicism in order to become king of Poland.

"Denkbild" is defined in some historical dictionaries as "monument" or "symbol" or "emblem," but none of these really makes

HISTORICALLY INFORMED RENDERING OF LIBRETTOS 105

sense here. "Rememorative image" perhaps best captures the sense. That is, "Denkbild" can be read as a shorter form of "Gedenkbild," which in turn can be read as a synonym for "Gedächtnisbild" ("memory image"). The aria's conceit, then, appears to be that "eternity's sapphiric house" is so magnificently emblazoned that the sight of the earth can no longer function as a reminder of its temporality.

Spotty or Missing Punctuation in the Original Bach Sources: Commas Can Really Matter

Strings of words can be genuinely ambiguous if they do not contain punctuation, and occasional spotty or missing punctuation in the original Bach sources has indeed sometimes generated confusion.

An example that has significant implications for interpretation is the opening couplet in the extremely well-known duet "Wir eilen mit schwachen, doch emsigen Schritten" from the cantata *Jesu, der du meine Seele* (BWV 78).

Bach's own score is lost, and his original performing part for soprano, copied out by an assistant, contains no punctuation at all in the duet, whereas his original performing part for alto contains exactly one comma and one period in this movement. There are always a great number of full and partial verbal repetitions in musical settings of aria poetry, and the punctuated bit here in question, at the end of the A section of the duet, reads in the original alto part, "wir eilen mit schwachen doch emsigen Schritten o Jesu o Meister zu helfen zu dir zu dir zu dir, wir eilen mit schwachen doch emsigen Schritten o Jesu o Meister zu helfen zu dir zu dir."

Traditionally, modern editors have punctuated the opening couplet of the duet as:

> Wir eilen mit schwachen, doch emsigen Schritten,
> O Jesu, o Meister, *zu helfen zu dir.*

106   TEXTS

But recently, there surfaced in Russia[67] a copy of the printed text booklet that was distributed to Bach's fellow congregants at the original performance of the cantata, and it gives the lines as:

> Wir eilen mit schwachen doch emsigen Schritten,
> O Jesu, o *Meister zu helfen*, zu dir.

Here, then, is an updated German text for the entire duet:

> Wir eilen mit schwachen, doch emsigen Schritten,
> O Jesu, o Meister zu helfen, zu dir.
>> Du suchest die Kranken und Irrenden treulich.
>> Ach höre, wie wir
>> Die Stimmen erheben, um Hülfe zu bitten!
>> Es sei uns dein gnädiges Antlitz erfreulich!

Crucial context for making proper sense of this movement is provided by the biblical portion that was read at the liturgical occasion for which Bach composed Cantata 78, namely, Luke 17:11–19, the story of "The Cleansing of Ten Lepers." In 17:13, the lepers are said to "lift up their voices" to Jesus, calling him "master," and in 17:19, Jesus responds, "Your faith [in God] has saved you." His response was rendered "dein Glaube hat dir *geholfen*" in the Luther Bibles known to Bach's original audiences. "Helfen" ("to help/assist") was one of Luther's many metaphors for "to save" (i.e., to save from a hellish life on earth and from an afterlife in hell), "to bring salvation."[68]

In Bach's cantata duet, Luke's language is taken up by the "ailing and erring," who "raise their voices" to Jesus and call him

---

[67] Tatjana Shabalina, "'Texte zur Music' in Sankt Petersburg: Weitere Funde," *Bach-Jahrbuch* 95 (2009): 11–48; a facsimile of Cantata 78's printed libretto is given at 38–39.

[68] The salvific metaphor in the underlying Greek text of Luke, however, is "sozo" ("to heal").

HISTORICALLY INFORMED RENDERING OF LIBRETTOS   107

"master." But they also call Jesus by an extended savior designation that has been eliminated, on account of comma placement, in many modern editions of Cantata 78. As mentioned earlier, these editions read: "*Wir eilen* mit schwachen, doch emsigen Schritten, o Jesu, o Meister, *zu helfen zu dir*" (literally, "*We hasten* with weak but diligent steps, oh Jesus, oh master, *to [be of] help to you*"). This is doctrinally topsy-turvy. Lutheran poetry would never rightly say that "the erring" can "help" Jesus, and many translators of this libretto have simply emended the passage (e.g., to "We hasten . . . *to you for help*") without necessarily realizing that they have done so.

As also mentioned earlier, the phrase "Meister, *zu helfen zu dir*" should instead read "*Meister zu helfen*, zu dir" (i.e., with its comma placed two words later). "Meister zu helfen" ("Master of Salvation"; literally, "master of help") was a commonplace title for Jesus in the Lutheran discourse of Bach's day.[69] The title originated from Isaiah 63:1 in the Luther Bible, where the bloodstained divine warrior— understood by Luther as the typological prefigurement of Jesus, the crucified Son of God—says, in Luther's idiosyncratic translation, "Ich bins, der Gerechtigkeit lehret und ein Meister bin zu helfen" ("I am the one who teaches righteousness, and am a master of help/salvation"). And so, while Cantata 78's duet may, at first glance, appear to be a simple plea for God's everyday help and assistance, it is, in fact, a prayer for eternal salvation, addressing Jesus as the "Meister zu helfen."

Here is a survey of how our five main translators have rendered the text of this movement, with italics marking the interpretively challenging words or strings of words:

---

[69] As discussed, e.g., in Renate Steiger, "Eine Predigt zum Locus De iustificatione: Die Kantate 'Jesu, der du meine Seele' BWV 78," in *Gnadengegenwart: Johann Sebastian Bach im Kontext lutherischer Orthodoxie und Frömmigkeit*, by Renate Steiger (Stuttgart-Bad Cannstatt: Frommann-Holzboog, 2002), 41–42.

108 TEXTS

UNGER[70]

(Wir eilen mit schwachen, doch emsigen Schritten,
O Jesu, o Meister, *zu helfen zu dir.*)

—

We hasten with weak, yet eager steps,
O Jesus, *O master, for help to thee.*
   Thou seekest the sick and erring faithfully.
   Ah, hear, how we
   (Our) voices raise, for *help* do entreat (thee)!
   (Now) be to-us thy gracious countenance gratifying!
   {May thy gracious countenance smile upon us!}

STOKES[71]

(Wir eilen mit schwachen, doch emsigen Schritten,
O Jesu, o Meister, *zu helfen zu dir.*)

—

We hasten with weak but diligent steps,
O Jesus, *O master, to Thee.*
   Thou seekest to *help* the ailing and erring.
   Ah, hearken, as we
   Raise our voices, to beg Thee for *help*!
   May Thy gracious countenance smile on us!

JONES[72]

(Wir eilen mit schwachen, doch emsigen Schritten,
O Jesu, o *Meister zu helfen*, zu dir.)

—

We hasten with weak yet eager steps,
 O Jesus, *O master, for help to You.*
   You faithfully seek the sick and straying
   Ah, hear how we

---

[70] Unger, *Handbook*, 273.
[71] Stokes, *Johann Sebastian Bach*, 129.
[72] Dürr, *The Cantatas*, trans. Jones, 523.

HISTORICALLY INFORMED RENDERING OF LIBRETTOS   109

Lift up our voices to pray for *help*!

May Your gracious countenance be gratifying to us!

AMBROSE[73]

(does not give the German source text)

–

We hasten with failing but diligent paces,

O Jesus, *O master, to thee for thy help.*

> Thou seekest the ailing and erring most faithful
> Ah, hearken, as we
> Our voices are raising to beg thee for *succor*!
> Let on us thy countenance smile ever gracious!

DELLAL[74]

(Wir eilen mit schwachen, doch emsigen Schritten,

O Jesu, o Meister, *zu helfen zu dir.*)

–

We hasten with weak, yet eager steps,

O Jesus, O Master, *to you for help.*

> You faithfully seek the ill and erring.
> Ah, hear, how we
> lift up our voices to beg for *help*!
> Let your gracious countenance be joyful to us!

We offer, then, the following translation as more closely and specifically capturing the salvifically centered sense of Cantata 78's poetry:

(Wir eilen mit schwachen, doch emsigen Schritten,

O Jesu, o *Meister zu helfen*, zu dir.)

–

We hasten with weak but diligent steps,

Oh Jesus, *oh Master of Salvation, to you.*

---

[73] Ambrose, *J. S. Bach*, 208.

[74] Dellal, "Bach Notes and Translations," https://www.emmanuelmusic.org/bach-translations/bwv-78.

110 TEXTS

You seek the ailing and erring faithfully,
Ah, hear, how we
Raise our voices to plead for *help/salvation.*
Let your merciful countenance be gladdening to us.[75]

Conclusion

Each of our new suggested renderings for the librettos from Bach's cantatas arises out of insights that depend upon knowledge of the broader linguistic, cultural, and religious contexts of Bach's music and the poetry he set. Unlike us moderns, Bach lived and worked in a biblically literate culture. We today cannot hope adequately to understand his (premodern) artistic output unless we aim to become historically informed about his religious *Sitz im Leben*, whatever our own predilections might be.[76]

APPENDIX: Parallel German-English Texts, with Annotations, of the Librettos from Two Church Cantatas and Two Secular Cantatas by Bach

To give an immediate and thorough sense of how various aspects of historically informed reading can affect one another within the parts of a libretto

---

[75] This line alludes to the priestly blessing of Israel in Numbers 6:24–26, rendered in the Luther Bibles of Bach's day as "Der HERR segne dich und behüte dich; der HERR lasse sein Angesicht leuchten über dir und sei dir gnädig; der HERR hebe sein Angesicht über dich, und gebe dir Frieden" ("The LORD bless you and protect you; the LORD let his countenance shine over you and be merciful to you; the LORD raise his countenance over you, and give you peace"). Luther understood this threefold blessing as Trinitarian: "The LORD [God the Father] bless . . .; the LORD [God the Son] let . . .; the LORD [God the Holy Spirit] raise . . ." There are extensive highlighting markings—as far as we know, they are Bach's—among the long commentaries on this passage in Bach's Calov Bible (which he acquired for his personal library apparently in the 1730s).

[76] This conclusion, appropriately, is nearly identical to the conclusion of the essay cited in the first footnote of this chapter.

HISTORICALLY INFORMED RENDERING OF LIBRETTOS 111

and also promote better understanding of the whole, we offer here four heavily annotated cantata translations, two of them liturgical works and two of them secular. These librettos were chosen because they are especially rich in historical, cultural, theological, linguistic, and text-critical issues. Notice, for example, that, contrary to typical modern expectation and typical Bach-scholarly reporting, the secular works also contain significant religious language.

We have rendered the German texts in modern spellings ("Tränen" in place of "Thränen," "beide" instead of "beyde," and so on) but kept original orthography where eighteenth-century usage suggests a different meaning from a word's rough modern equivalent and likewise where older spellings had extra letters that affected the poetry's scansion, a situation necessarily embodied in Bach's musical settings. We have also retained contractions (mostly dropped inflections at the ends of nouns and adjectives), which had been introduced by the poets most frequently to make lines of text fit the prescribed poetic meter. It is also worth noting that punctuation in the original sources is often nonexistent, spotty, wildly inconsistent, or simply baffling. To impart all the particulars would be tedious and futile. Usually, the immediate context's clues make matters clear enough, but sometimes our editorial decisions about punctuation, informed by non-obvious background considerations, differ significantly from those of other editors.

The notes on the English translations attempt to explain our choices in rendering the German texts in English, paying particular attention to eighteenth-century meanings and usages and to resonances (presumably intended) with scriptural texts in Luther's translation. We also aim to explain the Lutheran theological underpinnings of the cantata librettos on the assumption that listeners and readers of the time, unlike many today, would have understood Bach's cantata poetry in light of well-established doctrine.

The English versions attempt to preserve the line-by-line sense of the original, but the differences between German and English grammar sometimes make this impossible—or at least stylistically very awkward. Another inelegance stems from the fact that the English is meant to be read along with the German and not on its own, and so the English style and syntax will often leave something to be desired. Within a cantata, we have attempted to be consistent in translating words that appear several times in a work.

Following the conventions of cantata libretto printing, hymn texts are given here in bold type, biblical excerpts in italics, and recitatives and arias in roman type; formally distinct portions of text, such as a middle section of a da capo aria, are indented.

112 TEXTS

Wer Dank opfert, der preiset mich, BWV 17

Erster Teil   Part 1

1. *Wer Dank opfert, der preiset mich,*   1. *Whoever offers thanks, he praises*
und das[77] ist der Weg, dass ich ihm   *me [God]; and this is the way that*
zeige das Heil Gottes.[78]   *I [Jesus][79] show him the salvation of*
                                        God.

2. Es muss die ganze Welt ein stummer   2. The entire world [of nature] must
   Zeuge werden   become a mute witness
Von Gottes hoher Majestät,   To God's high majesty:
Luft, Wasser, Firmament und Erden,   Air, water, firmament, and earth,
Wenn ihre Ordnung als in Schnuren   As if their arrangement moves by
   geht;   puppet-string.[80]
Ihn preiset die Natur mit   Nature praises him by countless gifts
   ungezählten Gaben,
Die er ihr in den Schoss gelegt,   That he has placed in its bosom;[81]

---

[77] Some Luther Bibles of Bach's day here read "da" ("there"), not "das" ("this"); later and earlier Bibles also read "da." See also note 87, below.

[78] Psalm 50:23.

[79] The meaning of the received Hebrew text that underlies what the Luther Bibles have rendered "und da/das ist der Weg" is now uncertain. Most non-Lutheran renderings make it clear that the "I" in "I show him," just like the "me" of the opening phrase, refers to "God." The different form and content of these other renderings (e.g., "and to him who orders his conduct aright I will show the salvation of God" or "and to him who improves his way I will show the salvation of God") readily allow for the "I/me" to be "God" throughout the verse. But Luther would have rejected such translations on theological grounds, as he believed that humans could do nothing to merit being shown God's salvation. In the Lutheran interpretation of Bach's day, the voice of the psalmist here is the literal voice of the (preexistent) Christ himself, such that (the incarnated) Christ, Jesus, is then the one who shows/enacts the salvation of God.

[80] This line's phrase "in Schnuren geht" corresponds to the modern colloquialism "Es geht wie am Schnürchen" (literally, "it goes as [if] by the little [line of] string"). The expression can, among other things, refer to the controlling of puppets with strings. In Bach's cantata, then, "air, water, firmament, and earth" are like puppets: though speechless, they become expressive by dint of the way their controller moves them.

[81] The metaphor of the "Schoss" here is presumably not the "lap" but the archaic, biblical sense of "bosom," i.e., the enclosed space formed by one's chest and arms. The language of lines 5–6 and the sense that this refers to nature's "bosom" may be partly indebted to Proverbs 21:14, "Eine heimliche Gabe stillt den Zorn, und ein Geschenk im

HISTORICALLY INFORMED RENDERING OF LIBRETTOS   113

Und was den Odem hegt,	And that which enjoys[82] breath
Will noch mehr Anteil an	Desires to have still more portion
ihm haben,	in him,
Wenn es zu seinem Ruhm so	If [human] tongue as well as [bird]
Zung als Fittich regt.	wing[83] bestirs to his glory.

3. Herr, deine Güte reicht, so weit der Himmel ist,	3. Lord, your goodness reaches as far as the sky is,
Und deine Wahrheit langt, so weit die Wolken gehen.	And your truth extends as far as the clouds go.[84]
Wüsst ich gleich sonsten nicht, wie herrlich gross du bist,	If I did not yet know otherwise how gloriously great you are,
So könnt ich es gar leicht aus deinen Werken sehen.	I could so easily see it from your works [of Creation].[85]
Wie sollt man dich mit Dank davor nicht stetig preisen?	How shall one not, in return,[86] constantly praise you with thanks?
Da du uns willt den Weg des Heils hingegen weisen.	There [in your works], on the other hand [alongside your Word], you desire to show us the way of salvation.[87]

Schoss den heftigen Grimm" ("A secret gift stills anger, and a present in the bosom vehement wrath").

[82] "Hegen" is apparently being used here metaphorically in its archaic sense of "behagen" ("to enjoy"). The poet used the expression "was Odem hegt" ("that enjoys breath") in place of the standard biblical expression "was Odem hat" ("that has breath") to accommodate the poem's rhyme scheme.

[83] Apparently, the idea is not only that people and birds "desire" to glorify God but also that any glorifying of God will then be carried and repeated by others, by analogy to the way that rumors are carried and repeated by metaphorical "birds." The cryptic language of this line appears to be derived from Ecclesiastes 10:20, which in the Luther Bibles of Bach's day reads "die Vögel des Himmels führen die Stimme, und die Fittiche haben, sagens nach" ("the birds of the sky may carry [what] your voice [has expressed], and what has wings may repeat it").

[84] Lines 1–2 are a nearly verbatim quotation of Psalm 36:6 in the Luther Bibles of Bach's day, employed to go with the nature imagery of the previous movement.

[85] Seeing God's "works" and thus knowing God here refers not to his deeds in general but to nature—what God has made, the works of his Creation (as is expressed in Romans 1:20).

[86] "Davor" in older German, depending on context, can be simply an alternate spelling of "dafür" ("for this/in return"). "Dafür" is used in line 4 of movement 5.

[87] Here the meaning of the word "da" can be equivocal in the absence of taking into account that this line is a paraphrase of Psalm 50:23, the passage that appears verbatim

114 TEXTS

Zweiter Teil	Part 2

4. *Einer aber unter ihnen, da er sahe,*
dass er gesund worden war, kehrete um
und preiset Gott mit lauter Stimme
und fiel auf sein Angesicht zu seinen
Füssen und dankte ihm, und das war
ein Samariter.[88]

4. *But one among them [the lepers Jesus*
healed], when he saw that he had be-
come well, turned back [toward Jesus]
and praised God with a loud voice
and fell upon his face at his [Jesus's]
feet and thanked him—and this was a
Samaritan.[89]

5. Welch Übermass der Güte
Schenkst du mir!
Doch was gibt mein Gemüte
Dir dafür?
Herr, ich weiss sonst nichts zu
 bringen,
Als dir Dank und Lob zu singen.

5. What overmeasure of goodness
You bestow on me!
But what does my spirit
Give you in return?
Lord, I know nothing else to bring

But to sing you thanks and praise.

6. Sieh meinen Willen an, ich kenne,
 was ich bin:
Leib, Leben und Verstand,
Gesundheit, Kraft und Sinn,

6. Look upon my will; I know what
 I am:
Body, life, and understanding;[90]
health, strength, and mind;[91]

---

at the opening of the cantata. That verbatim text gives the contemporary biblical reading *"das* ist der Weg" (*"this* is the way"), but this paraphrase draws upon the alternative contemporary biblical wording "*da* ist der Weg" (*"there* is the way"); see also note 77, above.

[88] Luke 17:15–16.

[89] In the Lutheran view, it was especially remarkable, and laudable, that the only leper who thanked Jesus and praised God was a Samaritan, an inhabitant of the district of Samaria, the capital of the Northern Kingdom of Israel. The Lutheranism of Bach's day reckoned the Samaritans to be Gentiles ("Heiden") who worshiped pagan idols alongside the God of Israel; apparently, all the other lepers in the Luke 17 story were Jews.

[90] The life of the follower of Jesus is "the life of God," which according to Ephesians 4:18 is linked with proper "understanding" (in Luther Bibles, "Verstand").

[91] The mind of the follower of Jesus is "the mind of Christ," according to 1 Corinthians 2:16, which in the Luther Bibles of Bach's day reads, "Denn wer hat des HERRN Sinn erkannt? Oder wer will ihn unterweisen? Wir aber haben Christi Sinn" ("For who has known the mind of the LORD? Or who will instruct him? We [followers of Jesus], however, have the mind of Christ").

HISTORICALLY INFORMED RENDERING OF LIBRETTOS 115

Der[92] du mich lässt mit frohem Mund geniessen,	[All] of which you let me savor with enraptured mouth,
Sind Ströme deiner Gnad, die du auf mich lässt fliessen.	Are streams of your grace that you let flow upon me.
Lieb, Fried, Gerechtigkeit und Freud in deinem Geist	Love, peace, righteousness, and joy in your [Holy] Spirit[93]
Sind Schätz, dadurch du mir schon hier ein Vorbild weist,	Are treasures through which you show me now here [on earth] as a prefigurement
Was Gutes du gedenkst mir dorten zuzuteilen,	Of good things you have in mind to apportion me there [in heaven],
Um[94] mich an Leib und Seel vollkommentlich zu heilen.	So as to heal/save[95] me perfectly[96] in body and soul.

7. Wie sich ein Vatr erbarmet	7. Like a father has mercy
Übr seine junge Kindlein klein:	On his little young children:
So tut der Herr uns Armen,	The Lord acts in the same way toward us wretched ones
So wir ihn kindlich fürchten rein.	If we fear him innocently, childlike.

---

[92] Some modern editions silently change this "der" ("of which") to read "die" ("which").

[93] The language of this line is derived from Romans 14:17, which in the Luther Bibles of Bach's day reads, "das Reich Gottes ist . . . Gerechtigkeit und Friede, und Freude in dem Heiligen Geiste" ("the kingdom of God is righteousness and peace, and joy in the Holy Spirit"). The Calov Study Bible in Bach's personal library comments at this verse that the three best treasures of the kingdom of God are the righteousness of Christ, the peace with God the Father, and joy in the Holy Spirit.

[94] Modern editions here read "Und" ("And"). In Bach's own materials and in the libretto of this cantata reprinted in 1728, the line reads not "Und . . . zu heilen" ("And to heal/save") but "Um . . . zu heilen" ("So as to heal/save").

[95] This is the language of biblical typology. In this case, the good things of God in one's life on earth are "types" (i.e., prefigurements; biblical German, "Vorbilder") that foreshadow the good things of God in one's afterlife in heaven. The poet expertly equivocates in his use of the word "heilen" ("to heal" or "to save," or both), such that God's present good things on earth heal and save the believer, and then God's future good things, the "antitypes," effect and reflect the perfection of salvation experienced in heaven (see also note 96, below).

[96] This line draws upon 1 Corinthians 13:10, "Wenn aber kommen wird das Vollkommene, so wird das Stückwerk aufhören" ("But when what is perfect [the heavenly] will come, then what is piecemeal [the earthly] will leave off").

116 TEXTS

Er kennt das arme Gemächte,	He knows the wretched creature;
Gott weiss, wir sind nur Staub.	We are, Lord knows,[97] but dust.
Gleichwie das Gras vom Rechen,	Just like grass to the rake,
Ein Blum und fallendes Laub,	Like a flower and falling foliage,
Der Wind nur drüber wehet,	The wind merely wafts over it,
So ist es nimmer da:	And it is there no more:[98]
Also der Mensch vergehet,	In the same way, the human being passes;
Sein End, das ist ihm nah.[99]	His end, it is near.

Angenehmes Wiederau, BWV 30.1
(formerly BWV 30a)

1. (*Zeit, Glück, Elster, Schicksal*)	1.[100] (*Time, Fortune, the River Elster,*[101] *Fate*)
Angenehmes Wiederau,	Pleasant [manor of] Wiederau,[102]
Freue dich in deinen Auen!	Rejoice over your meadows.[103]
Das Gedeihen legt itzund	Flourishing now lays

---

[97] The expression "Gott weiss" (literally, "God knows") is used here not as an affirmation of the omniscience of God. It simply emphasizes the truth and obviousness of what is being said; just as, e.g., in English, one might say "Lord/Goodness/God knows I need a haircut."

[98] This line's "ist es nimmer da" does not mean "it is never there." Here "nimmer" is an older German form of "nicht mehr"; later German might use "nimmermehr."

[99] A stanza of "Sei Lob und Preis mit Ehren."

[100] It is perhaps worth mentioning that this cantata libretto is extraordinarily difficult to translate, as the German text shows all signs of having been written rather hastily and carelessly.

[101] The "[White] Elster River" was near the "Wiederau" country estate (see note 102, below).

[102] Wiederau was a "Rittergut" ("manor") about fourteen miles south of Leipzig. This cantata was composed for the celebrations surrounding the installation in 1737 of Johann Christian von Hennicke (1681–1752) as new owner and lord of the Wiederau manor, which had been built on low, soft ground near the White Elster River.

[103] The sense of the line is not "Go out into your meadows and rejoice there," as some published translations suggest or might imply.

HISTORICALLY INFORMED RENDERING OF LIBRETTOS   117

Einen neuen festen Grund,	Its new secure foundation,[104]
Wie ein Eden dich zu bauen.	To tend[105] you [Wiederau] as an Eden.[106]

2. (*Schicksal*)	2. (*Fate*)
So ziehen wir	Thus we gather[107] here
In diesem Hause hier	In this house,
Mit Freuden ein;	With joy;
Nichts soll uns hier von dannen reissen.	Nothing shall tear [those of] us here away from there.
Du bleibst zwar, schönes Wiederau,	You remain, indeed, lovely Wiederau,
Der Anmut Sitz, des Segens Au;	Charm's seat, blessing's meadow.
Allein	But
(*Zeit, Glück, Elster, Schicksal*)	(*Time, Fortune, the River Elster, Fate*)
Dein Name soll geändert sein,	Your name shall be changed;
Du sollst nun Hennicks-Ruhe heissen!	You shall now be called[108] "Hennicke's[109] Tranquility."
(*Schicksal*)	(*Fate*)
Nimm dieses Haupt, dem du nun untertan,	This master [Hennicke], to whom you are now subject,

[104] This is probably, in part, an allusion to the Wiederau estate's location on insecure ground (see note 102, above) and the need for an elaborate pile foundation to ensure stability.

[105] The verb "bauen" in this context means not "to build" but "to tend" or "to cultivate"; see note 106, below.

[106] This sentiment is apparently adapted from Genesis 2:15, which in the Luther Bibles of Bach's day reads, "Und Gott der HERR nahm den Menschen und setzte ihn in den Garten Eden, dass er ihn baut und bewahrt" ("And God the LORD took the man [that he had created, Adam] and put him into the garden, Eden, that he [Adam] might tend and ward it [the garden]").

[107] The verb "einziehen," with dative (where accusative might have been expected?), seems to be used here in the sense of "to draw together" or "to gather."

[108] This language is apparently based on the common biblical formula "du sollst nicht mehr [X] heissen, sondern [Y]" ("you shall no longer be called [X] but [Y]"), for example, in Genesis 17:5, 17:15, 32:28, 35:10; Isaiah 47:5, 62:4. Such language in the cantata apparently suggests divine blessing.

[109] Regarding "Hennicke," see note 102, above.

118 TEXTS

Frohlockend also an:	Thus accept exultantly:

3. (*Schicksal*)

3. (*Fate*)

Willkommen im Heil, willkommen in Freuden,	Be welcome in prosperity,[110] be welcome in joy;
Wir segnen die Ankunft, wir segnen das Haus.	[Hennicke,] we bless your arrival, we bless your house.
Sei stets wie unsre Auen munter,	Be ever hale like our meadows;
Dir[111] breiten sich die Herzen unter,	[Our] hearts submit themselves to you,
Die Allmacht aber Flügel aus.	But [God's] omnipotence[112] spreads [its] wings over you.[113]

4. (*Glück*)

4. (*Fortune*)

Da heute dir, gepriesner Hennicke,	Because today,[114] vaunted Hennicke,
Dein Wiedrau sich verpflicht,	Your Wiederau pledges itself to you,
So schwör[115] auch ich,	So I [Fortune], too, swear
Dir unveränderlich	To be unvaryingly
Getreu und hold zu sein.	Faithful and kind to you.
Ich wanke nicht, ich weiche nicht,	I do not waver, I do not yield

---

[110] The noun "Heil" has a wide variety of meanings; in this libretto, it is apparently used in its general sense of "Wohlstand" ("prosperity").

[111] The printed libretto distributed to the original audience reads "hier" ("here"), but Bach's score and original performing part read "dir" ("to you").

[112] "Die Allmacht" means "the omnipotence [of God]." The German equivalent of "the Almighty" (a name for God) would be "der Allmächtige."

[113] Literally, the last two lines would read, "The hearts spread themselves under you, but omnipotence spread[s] wings over you." The challenge is that the poet uses two separable verbs with a common root: "*unter*breiten" ("to submit to"; hyperliterally, "to spread under") and "*aus*breiten" ("to spread over"). The poet's grammar is not pristine, either. The separable "breiten" is plural and here has to do work for "die Herzen" (plural, "the hearts") and "die Allmacht" (singular, "the omnipotence"); i.e., the latter requires "brei*tet* ... aus," not "[brei*ten*] ... aus."

[114] This cantata was performed on Saturday, September 28, 1737, at an "Erbhuldigung," a feudal ceremony in which an oath of fealty was sworn by subjects upon the arrival of a new manorial lord.

[115] Both the printed libretto distributed to the original audience and the original Bach sources read "schwer," which is simply an older spelling of "schwör."

HISTORICALLY INFORMED RENDERING OF LIBRETTOS   119

An deine Seite mich zu binden.	In binding myself to your side.
Du sollst mich allenthalben finden.	You shall find me everywhere.

5. (*Glück*)	5. (*Fortune*)
Was die Seele kann ergötzen,	That which the soul can enjoy,
Was vergnügt und hoch zu schätzen,	That which pleases and is to be highly cherished,
Soll dir lehn[116] und erblich sein.	Shall be manorial[117] and hereditary to you.
Meine Fülle soll nichts sparen	My abundance shall spare nothing
Und dir reichlich offenbaren,	And shall richly reveal to you
Dass mein ganzer Vorrat dein.	That my whole store [of fortune is] yours.

6. (*Schicksal*)	6. (*Fate*)
Und wie ich jederzeit bedacht	And just as I have ever been mindful,
Mit aller Sorg und Macht,	With all care and might,
Weil du es wert bist, dich zu schützen	To protect you, because you are worthy of it,
Und wider alles dich zu unterstützen,	And to support you against all things,
So hör ich auch nicht ferner auf,	So I will also henceforth not cease
Vor dich zu wachen	To watch over you,
Und deines Ruhmes Ehrenlauf	And to make your renown's path of honor
Erweiterter und blühender zu machen.	More extended and more thriving.

---

[116] In Bach's handwriting, it is often unclear whether the "L" at the beginning of a word is uppercase or lowercase. Modern editions of the cantata give "Lehn" (a noun) here, but the printed libretto distributed to the original audience gives "lehn" (an adjective), understood as a clipped version of "lehnbar" ("feudal/manorial"). The adjectives "lehn" and "erblich" in this line would correspond to the dedication formulation on the title page of the original printed libretto: "dem . . . Johann Christian von Hennicke, Erb- Lehn- und Gerichts-Herr auf Wiederau" ("to . . . Johann Christian von Hennicke, Hereditary Lord, Feudal/Manorial Lord, and Justice of the Peace [literally, "Tribunal Lord"] in Wiederau").

[117] On this word being an adjective, see note 116, above.

120 TEXTS

7. (*Schicksal*)

Ich will dich halten
Und mit dir walten,

Wie man ein Auge zärtlich hält.
Ich habe dein Erhöhen,
Dein Heil und Wohlergehen
Auf Marmorsäulen aufgestellt.

7. (*Fate*)

I will sustain you
And will preside [over Wiederau] with you,

Just as one fondly keeps an eye out.
I have raised your elevation,
Your prosperity and welfare,
On marble columns.[118]

8. (*Zeit*)

Und obwohl sonst der Unbestand

Mit mir verschwistert und verwandt,
So sei hiermit doch zugesagt:
So oft die Morgenröte tagt,
So lang ein Tag den andern folgen lässt,
So lange will ich steif und fest,
Mein Hennicke, dein Wohl
Auf meine Flügel ferner bauen.

Dich soll die Ewigkeit zuletzt,
Wenn sie mir selbst die Schranken setzt,
Nach mir noch übrig schauen.

8. (*Time*)

And though otherwise inconstancy [is]

Sibling and kindred to me,
Let it hereby nonetheless be agreed:
As often as the daybreak dawns,
As long as one day is followed by the next,
This long do I wish absolutely,
My Hennicke, [for] your well-being
To rest henceforth on my wings ["of time"].

In the end, eternity shall—
When it sets its limits even on me—
Continue after me to watch [over you].

9. (*Zeit*)

Eilt, ihr Stunden, wie ihr wollt,
Rottet aus und stosst zurücke!
Aber merket dies allein,
Dass ihr diesen Schmuck und Schein,

9. (*Time*)

Hasten, you hours, as you wish;
Wipe out and knock [things] back.
But just take note of this:
That this finery and luster,

---

[118] The "marble columns" metaphor is probably meant to suggest that Fate will see to the manorial lord's immortality.

HISTORICALLY INFORMED RENDERING OF LIBRETTOS 121

Dass ihr Hennicks Ruhm und Glücke
Allezeit verschonen sollt!

That Hennicke's renown and fortune,
You shall always spare.

10. (*Elster*)
So recht! ihr seid mir werte Gäste.

Ich räum euch Au und Ufer ein.
Hier bauet eure Hütten
Und eure Wohnung feste;
Hier wollt, hier sollet ihr beständig
sein!
Vergesset keinen Fleiss,
All eure Gaben haufenweis
Auf diese Fluren auszuschütten!

10. (*The River Elster*)
Right so! You [Wiederau] are my
esteemed guests.
I cede meadow and riverbank to you.
Here build your dwellings
And your abode securely;
Here you would—here you shall—be
long-enduring.
Forget no effort
In pouring out all your gifts heapingly
Upon these fields.

11. (*Elster*)
So, wie ich die Tropfen zolle,
Dass mein Wiedrau grünen solle,
So fügt auch euern Segen bei!

Pfleget sorgsam Frucht und Samen,
Zeiget, dass euch Hennicks Namen
Ein ganz besonders Kleinod sei!

11. (*The River Elster*)
Just as I vouchsafe[119] drops [of water],
That my Wiederau may grow verdant,
So [I command you to] add also your
blessings:
Carefully cultivate fruit and seeds;
Show that to you Hennicke's name
Is a very special gem.

12. (*Zeit*)
Drum, angenehmes Wiederau,
Soll dich kein Blitz, kein Feuerstrahl,
Kein ungesunder Tau,
Kein Misswachs, kein Verderben
schrecken!

12. (*Time*)
Thus, pleasant Wiederau,
No lightning, no thunderbolt,
No unhealthy dew,
No crop failure, no [crop] spoilage
shall alarm you.

---

[119] Normally, "zollen" means "to pay taxes," but in poetry, the verb was often used simply as a synonym for "geben" ("to give") or "gewähren" ("to vouchsafe"), as the various forms of "zollen" accommodated many quick rhyme schemes.

122 TEXTS

(*Schicksal*)	(*Fate*)
Dein Haupt, den teuren Hennicke,	Your master, the precious Hennicke,
Will ich mit Ruhm und Wonne decken.	I will bedeck with renown and gladness.
(*Glück*)	(*Fortune*)
Dem wertesten Gemahl	The most esteemed wife [Sophia Elisabeth][120]
Will ich kein Heil und keinen Wunsch versagen,	Will I deny no prosperity and no wish.
(*Zeit, Glück, Elster, Schicksal*)	(*Time, Fortune, the River Elster, Fate*)[121]
Und beider Lust,[122]	And the delight of both [husband and wife],
Den einigen und liebsten Stamm, August,	The only and most beloved scion, [their son] August,[123]
Will ich auf meinem Schosse tragen.	I will bear upon my bosom.
13. (*Zeit, Glück, Elster, Schicksal*)	13. (*Time, Fortune, the River Elster, Fate*)
Angenehmes Wiederau,	Pleasant Wiederau,
Prange nun in deinen Auen!	Boast[124] now over your meadows.[125]

---

[120] The dative formulation "*dem* Gemahl" could refer to a male or female spouse, but the context here dictates that it refers to Hennicke's wife, Countess Sophia Elisabeth, née (von) Götze (1686–1749). "*Das* Gemahl" can mean "the wife" or "the bride"; "*der* Gemahl" can mean "the husband" or "the lord" or "the male consort of a female monarch"; and "die Gemahlin" means "the female consort of a male monarch."

[121] Modern editions of the libretto often indicate that only Time, Fortune, and Fate sing here, but in fact, the River Elster joins them.

[122] The printed libretto distributed to the original audience reads "Und beider Augen-Lust" ("And the eyes' delight of both [husband and wife]").

[123] Their only son, Friedrich August von Hennicke (1720–1753), heir of the Wiederau manor. It is often mistakenly suggested that the "August" in this poem refers to the ruler who was called "Friedrich August II" as elector of Saxony and "Augustus III" as king of Poland. (This ruler was Friedrich August von Hennicke's namesake.)

[124] "Prangen" seems to be used here in its sense as a synonym for "prahlen" ("to show off," "to boast").

[125] The sense of the line is not "Go out into your meadows now and be resplendent there," as some published translations suggest or might imply.

HISTORICALLY INFORMED RENDERING OF LIBRETTOS   123

Deines Wachstums Herrlichkeit,	Of the glory of your increase,
Deiner Selbstzufriedenheit	Of your heart's content,
Soll die Zeit kein Ende schauen!	Time shall see no end.

Christian Friedrich Henrici[126]

Mein Herze schwimmt im Blut, BWV 199

1. Mein Herze schwimmt im Blut,	1.[127] My heart floats in [congested] blood,[128]
Weil mich der Sünden Brut	Because sin's brood[129]
In Gottes heilgen Augen	Makes me into a monster
Zum Ungeheuer macht.	In God's holy eyes;
Und mein Gewissen fühlet Pein,	And my conscience feels pain,
Weil mir die Sünden nichts	Because sins, to me, are nothing
Als Höllenhenker sein.	But hell's executioners.
Verhasste Lasternacht,	Hateful vice's night,[130]
Du, du allein	You, you alone
Hast mich in solche[131] Not gebracht;	Have brought me into such distress;

[126] Henrici was the librettist for several Bach works, and because his name is among the supporters listed on the title page of the printed libretto that was distributed to the original audience, it is assumed that he was the librettist.

[127] For an extremely illuminating discussion, rich in religious, cultural, and medical observations about this cantata, see Bettina Varwig, "Heartfelt Musicking: The Physiology of a Bach Cantata," *Representations* 143, no. 1 (2018): 36–62.

[128] It is not wrong to translate "schwimmt" as "swims," but here the word needs to be understood in the sense of "to passively float on the surface of a liquid," not "to actively move in, or on, a liquid." In Bach's day, the idea that one's heart might float in blood—indicating an imbalance of blood, one of the four humors—was connected with sadness, and the initiating cause of this condition was held to be sin (see also note 129, below).

[129] "Sin" here is singular (with its "n" ending, characteristic of older German), not plural. The word refers to the Lutheran belief in "original sin," the condition of human nature's essence being corrupted as a result of Adam and Eve disobeying God in the Garden of Eden. Sinful acts are the "brood/offspring" of original sin.

[130] Drunkenness and other unnamed vices are associated with "the night" in 1 Thessalonians 5:4–8, where it is said that the followers of Jesus are "not of the night, nor of darkness."

[131] In the poet's printed version of 1711, this reads not "solche Not" ("such distress") but "diese Not" ("this distress").

124 TEXTS

Und du, du böser Adamssamen,	And you, you evil seed [sown in the heart] of Adam,[132]
Raubst meiner Seelen alle Ruh	Rob my soul of all rest
Und schliessest ihr den Himmel zu!	And close ["rainfall" from] heaven[133] to it [my soul].
Ach! unerhörter Schmerz!	Ah, unheard-of agony!
Mein ausgedorrtes Herz	Henceforward no consolation will water
Will ferner mehr kein Trost befeuchten,[134]	My dried-up heart,[135]
Und ich muss mich vor dem verstecken,	And I must hide myself from him [God],
Vor dem die Engel selbst ihr Angesicht verdecken.	Before whom even the angels cover their faces.[136]
2. Stumme Seufzer, stille Klagen,	2. Mute sighs, silent lamentations,
Ihr mögt meine Schmerzen sagen,	You may speak of my agonies,
Weil der Mund geschlossen ist.	Because my mouth is closed.[137]

[132] This somewhat cryptic line probably refers also to "original sin" (see note 129, above). "Du böser Adamssamen" apparently does not mean "you evil seed of Adam" in the sense of "you evil progeny of Adam" (i.e., "you sinners, who are the descendants of Adam"). The sense is most likely "you evil seed sown in the heart of Adam," as the cantata's expression "evil seed" seems to be derived specifically from 2 Esdras 4:30, "Denn in dem Herzen Adams ist von Anfang gesät ein Korn böses Samens; wie viel gottloses Dinges hat es bis hierher gebracht" ("For in the heart of Adam was sown from the beginning a grain of evil seed; thus far, how much ungodliness has it [this grain of evil seed] brought"). The books of Esdras were included in some Luther Bibles of Bach's day.

[133] "Shutting/Closing up the skies/heavens" such that there is no rainfall is a stock expression in the Hebrew Bible. In the cantata, the notion is that sin dries up the heart, and only God can water the heart, with consolation, by opening up the blessedness of heaven to it.

[134] Some modern editions mistakenly give the verb "befruchten" ("to fertilize/fructify") for "befeuchten" ("to water").

[135] It is the hellish heat of sin that dries up the heart.

[136] As stated in Isaiah 6:2.

[137] The "I" in the cantata, with a "closed mouth," is being likened to the writer of Psalm 38, who as a helpless sinner remains silent and waits for God because he has no way to withstand evil by himself. The language of this line is derived specifically from Luther's idiosyncratic rendering of Psalm 38:14, "Ich aber muss sein . . . wie ein Stummer, der

HISTORICALLY INFORMED RENDERING OF LIBRETTOS   125

Und ihr nassen Tränenquellen	And you wet springs of tears
Könnt ein sichres Zeugnis stellen,	Can give sure witness
Wie mein sündlich Herz gebüsst.	Of how my sinful heart has repented.
Mein Herz ist itzt ein Tränenbrunn,	My heart is now a well of tears,[138]
Die Augen heisse Quellen.	My eyes hot springs.
Ach Gott! wer wird dich doch	Ah, God, who will yet satisfy[139] you?
zufriedenstellen?	

3. Doch Gott muss mir genädig sein,	3. Yet God must be gracious to me,
Weil ich das Haupt mit Asche,	Because I wash my head with ashes[140]
Das Angesicht mit Tränen wasche,	[And] my countenance with tears,
Mein Herz in Reu und Leid	[And because I] shatter my heart[141] in
zerschlage	remorse and suffering
Und voller Wehmut sage:	And say, full of melancholy:

seinen Mund nicht auftut" ("But I [as a helpless sinner] have to be like a mute person, who [cannot respond to his foes and thus] does not open his mouth").

[138] For the heart to "float in blood" is not a good thing (see note 128, above). The liquid in which the heart floats ought, instead, to move about through the body. Thus, this cantata poetry, conflating congested blood and tears, speaks of "springs of wet tears" flowing from "the heart [that is] a well of tears" and then streaming out from the "eyes [that are] hot springs."

[139] "Satisfy" is meant here in its technical sense of "to make atonement [for sin]" (i.e., where "Zufriedenstellung" is a synonym for "Versöhnung"), not in its more informal sense of "to fulfill a desire." The cantata's question is presumably a rhetorical one, as the Lutheran understanding, overwhelmingly, was that only Christ can satisfy God the Father.

[140] "Ashes" here apparently do double duty as symbols of sadness and of cleansing. Putting ashes on one's head was a gesture of grief, portrayed in several key biblical narratives (e.g., 2 Samuel 13:19, Ezekiel 27:30, and the expanded Greek version of Esther 3:2 [14:2 in modern English Bibles]). To "*wash* with ashes" might sound strange to modern readers, but audiences in Bach's day would more likely have known about "Lauge" ("lye") as a liquid that was leached from wood ashes and employed for making soap.

[141] The notion of a shattered heart is derived from Psalm 51:19, which in the Luther Bibles of Bach's day reads, "Die Opfer, die Gott gefallen, sind ein geängster Geist: ein geängstes und zerschlagen Herz wirst du, Gott, nicht verachten" ("The offerings that please God are [not burnt animal sacrifices but] a distressed spirit: a distressed and shattered heart, God, you will not despise").

"Gott sei mir Sünder gnädig!"

Ach ja! sein Herze bricht,

Und meine Seele spricht:

"God, be gracious to me the sinner."[142]

Ah, yes, his heart breaks [for me],[143]

And my soul says:

4. Tief gebückt und voller Reue

Lieg ich, liebster Gott, vor dir.

Ich bekenne meine Schuld,

Aber habe doch Geduld,

Habe doch Geduld mit mir!

4. Deeply bent over[144] and full of remorse

I lie, dearest God, before you.

I acknowledge my guilt,

But [may you] yet have patience,

Yet have patience with me.

5. Auf diese Schmerzensreu

Fällt mir alsdenn dies Trostwort bei:

5. Then, upon this aching remorse,

This word of consolation comes to mind:[145]

6. Ich, dein betrübtes Kind,

Werf alle meine Sünd,

So viel ihr in mir stecken

Und mich so heftig schrecken,

In deine tiefen Wunden,

6. I, your [Jesus's] dejected child,

Cast all my sins,

So many of them as stick fast within me

And frighten me so grievously,[146]

Into your deep wounds,[147]

---

[142] A quotation of Luke 18:13, from the gospel portion chanted on the occasion that this cantata was designed for. The original Greek of Luke's phrase ends "me *the* sinner," not "me[,] *a* sinner."

[143] The sense of this line is apparently derived from Luther's idiosyncratic rendering of Jeremiah 31:20, "darum bricht mir mein Herz gegen ihn, dass ich mich sein erbarmen muss, spricht der HERR" ("therefore my heart breaks for him [Ephraim], so that I must have mercy on him, says the LORD").

[144] The sense of this line is dependent on Psalm 38:7 in the Luther Bibles of Bach's day, where the psalmist, weighed down by sin, says, "Ich gehe krumm und sehr gebückt; den ganzen Tag gehe ich traurig" ("I go about hunched and very bent over; all the day I go about, mournful").

[145] "Etwas fallen jemandem bei" is an older German synonym for "etwas fallen jemandem ein," in the sense of "something comes to one's mind."

[146] That is, frighten me with the prospect of eternal damnation.

[147] Regarding "the wounds [of Jesus]," see note 149, below.

HISTORICALLY INFORMED RENDERING OF LIBRETTOS   127

Da ich stets Heil gefunden.[148]

Where I have always found salvation.

7. Ich lege mich in diese Wunden

Als in den rechten Felsenstein;

Die sollen meine Ruhstatt sein.

In diese will ich mich im Glauben
   schwingen

Und drauf vergnügt und fröhlich
   singen:

7. I lay myself into these wounds

As into [Christ] the proper quarry
   stone;[149]

They [the wounds] shall be my place
   of rest.

Into these [wounds] will I, in
   [Christian] belief,[150] fling myself

And thereupon contentedly and
   cheerfully sing:

---

[148] A stanza of "Wo soll ich fliehen hin."

[149] This notion of a "proper stone" is presumably derived from the quotation of Psalm 118:26 famously applied to Jesus in Acts 4:11: "[Jesus] ist der Stein, von euch Bauleuten verworfen, der zum Eckstein worden ist" ("[the apostle Peter said to the people of Israel: 'Jesus] is the stone, rejected by you builders, that/who is become the cornerstone' "); Psalm 118:26 is similarly quoted in Matthew 21:42, Mark 12:10, Luke 20:17, and 1 Peter 2:7. But the cantata's phrase "in den . . . Felsenstein" is also, further, an adaptation of poetic language from the Hebrew Bible that had come to be associated with the wounds of the crucified Jesus. In the call of the lover to his beloved in Song of Songs 2:14, "Meine Taube in den Felslöchern, in den Steinritzen" ("My dove [ensconced] in the cliff hollows, in the rock clefts, [let me see you]"), the dove was taken to foreshadow the church, and the rock cavities were taken to foreshadow the wounds in the side of Jesus's body that are narrated in John 19:34, "Der Kriegsknechte einer eröffnete seine Seite mit einem Speer, und alsobald ging Blut und Wasser heraus" ("[Upon seeing that Jesus was dead on the cross,] one of the Roman soldiers opened his [Jesus's] side with a spear, and immediately blood and water went out"). The wound cavity in Jesus's rib was embraced as a metaphorical place of refuge for Christian believers, as, for example, here in line 3 of the cantata poetry; for another example, consider a chorale stanza in the Wagner Hymnal, owned by Bach, which reads: "Jesu, . . . / Deiner Wunden Höhle / Ist mein Aufenthalt / . . . [Ich] finde Ruh / In der offnen Seiten Ritze / Da ich sicher sitze" ("Jesus, . . . your wound cavity is my abode . . . I find rest/peace in the opened side's cleft, where I sit securely").

[150] The language of "Glauben" ("[Christian] faith/belief") and of "legen in" ("to lay [something] into [something]") here is derived from John 20:27, which in the Luther Bibles of Bach's day reads, "Spricht er zu Thomas: . . . reiche deine Hand her und lege sie in meine Seite, und sei nicht ungläubig, sondern gläubig" ("He [Jesus] says to Thomas [the disciple]: Reach your hand here [in this loose garment] and lay it into my side [where there is a hollow from my spear wound on the cross], and be not unbelieving [in me as God's Messiah] but believing").

128 TEXTS

8. Wie freudig ist mein Herz,	8. How joyful is my heart,
Da Gott versöhnet ist.	Because God is reconciled [to the sinner by Christ's wounds];
Und mir nach[151] Reu und Leid	And [because] after [my] remorse and suffering,
Nicht mehr die Seligkeit	[God] will not any longer close[152] [eternal] blessedness
Noch auch sein Herz verschliesst.	Or his heart to me.

Georg Christian Lehms

Tönet, ihr Pauken! Erschallet, Trompeten!, BWV 214

DRAMA / PER MUSICA, / Welches / Bei dem Allerhöchsten / Geburts- Feste / Der / Allerdurchlauchtigsten und Gross- / mächtigsten / Königin in Polen / und / Churfürstin zu Sachsen / in unterthänigster Ehrfurcht / aufgeführet wurde / in dem / COLLEGIO MUSICO / Durch / J. S. B.	Musical drama, which was performed on the most elevated birthday celebration of the most serene and most mighty Queen of Poland and Electress of Saxony in most submissive reverence in the Collegium Musicum by J. S. B.
1. *Irene. Bellona. Pallas. Fama*[153] Tönet, ihr Pauken! Erschallet, Trompeten! Klingende Saiten, erfüllet die Luft!	1. Sound forth, you drums; ring out, trumpets. Sonorous strings, fill the air.

---

[151] Bach wrote "auf Reu und Leid" ("upon remorse and suffering") in bar 19 of his own score (which is the same wording as the poet's printed text of 1711), but then wrote "nach Reu und Leid" ("after remorse and suffering") in bars 23 and 26.

[152] On God's closing of heaven/blessedness, see note 133, above.

[153] Irene is the Greek goddess of peace (Pax to the Romans); Bellona is the Roman goddess of war; Pallas Athena (Minerva to the Romans) is the Greek goddess of war,

HISTORICALLY INFORMED RENDERING OF LIBRETTOS 129

Singet itzt Lieder, ihr muntren Poeten, Sing songs now, you blithe poets,
Königin lebe! wird fröhlich geruft. "Long live the Queen!" is cheerfully
called out.
Königin lebe! dies wünschet der "Long live the Queen!"—the Saxon
Sachse, wishes this;
Königin lebe und blühe und wachse! "Long live the Queen and blossom
and flourish!"[154]

2. *Irene*: Heut ist der Tag, 2. Today is the day
Wo jeder sich erfreuen mag. On which everyone may rejoice.
Dies ist der frohe Glanz This is the cheerful splendor
Der Königin Geburts-Fests-Stunden, Of the Queen's birthday-celebration
hours
Die Polen, Sachsen und uns ganz That have found Poles, Saxons, and
all of us
In grösster Lust und Glück erfunden. In greatest delight and fortune.
Mein Ölbaum My olive tree
Kriegt so Saft als fetten Raum. Yields[155] both oil and rich ointment;[156]

wisdom, weaving, and chastity; Fama (Pheme, or Rumor to the Romans) was the Greek
personification of fame, renown, and rumor. In this Drama per Musica for the birthday
of Maria Josepha (1699–1757), Saxon electress and queen of Poland, on December 8,
1733, all four speaking characters are female.

[154] The words rendered here in quotation marks are in larger type in the printed libretto that was distributed to Bach's original audience, probably implying that these are
to be understood as quoted words. In movement 7, the words "Kron und Preis gekrönter
Damen!" are printed the same way, as is the last line of the cantata, "Königin, lebe, ja lebe
noch lang." All these, too, are presumably to be understood as quoted words. The libretto
also usually singles out "Königin," "Sachsen," and "Polen," presumably for respectful emphasis rather than as quotations.

[155] Here "kriegen" is an archaic synonym for "gewinnen" ("to yield"). This is the way
the word was used, for example, in Psalm 107:37, which in the Luther Bibles of Bach's
day reads, "Weinberge pflanzen möchten, und die Jährliche Früchte kriegeten" ("[they]
might plant vineyards, and might yield the yearly fruit").

[156] In this context, "fetten Raum" does not mean "spacious room" or "fertile ground."
"Raum" is an archaic synonym for "Rahm" ("milk cream," here a metaphor for "olive
cream" or "ointment"), employed to effect a rhyme with "Baum." Irene, the goddess of
peace (see note 153, above), speaks of the olive tree because it is a symbol of peace; her
tree is extremely fecund and therefore well able to foster peace.

130 TEXTS

Er zeigt noch keine falbe Blätter;	It shows yet no pallid leaves;
Mich schreckt kein Sturm, Blitz,	No storm, lightning, dark clouds,
trübe Wolken, düstres Wetter.	gloomy weather frightens me.

3. *Bellona*: Blast die wohlgegriffnen Flöten,	3. Blow the well-fingered flutes[157]
Dass Feind, Lilien, Mond erröten!	So that enemy, fleur-de-lis,[158] moon[159] may blush;[160]
Schallt mit jauchzendem Gesang!	Make noise [you flutes] with jubilant song;
Tönt mit eurem Waffenklang!	Sound forth with your weaponry clangor.[161]
Dieses Fest erfordert Freuden,	This celebration calls for joys
Die so Geist als Sinnen weiden.	That feed both spirit and senses.

4. *Bellona*: Mein knallendes Metall,	4. My roaring metal
Der in der Luft erbebenden	Of the air-quaking
Cartauen;[162]	demicannons,[163]
Der frohe Schall;	The joyous noise,

---

[157] "Blasen" ("blow") and "griffen" (literally, "grip") are the verbs used for the playing of woodwind instruments. "Fingering charts," indicating which holes to cover to produce each of the notated pitches in an instrument's range, are called "Grifftabellen" (literally, "grip tables") in German.

[158] "Lilien," here, is a reference to "die drei Lilien" ("the three lilies") of the fleur-de-lis that was used by the French as a symbol of their kingdom. The libretto of Bach's Cantata 215 claims that Saxony is fortunate, in the face of the threatening "power of the French," to have Maria Josepha and her husband as rulers.

[159] "Mond," here, is a reference to the "Halbmond" ("crescent moon") used by the Turks as a symbol of their power. The librettos of Bach's Cantatas 18 and 126 express strong contempt for Turks.

[160] In one of its early-eighteenth-century uses, the flute was strongly associated with the military and military men, and its sound might thus be expected to discomfit enemies.

[161] Cantata 215 also connects flutes with weaponry.

[162] To make a cleaner rhyme with "Schauen," the original sources employed not "Cartaunen" or "Carthaunen" but the alternative spelling "Carthauen."

[163] Technically, the "Cartaune"—from the Latin "quartana" ("of the fourth size")—was shorter and smaller than what was called a "Kanone" ("cannon"). In eighteenth-century England, the artillery piece analogous to the Cartaune was called a "demicannon."

HISTORICALLY INFORMED RENDERING OF LIBRETTOS   131

Das angenehme Schauen;	The pleasant spectacle,
Die Lust, die Sachsen itzt empfindt,	The delight that Saxony now feels,
Rührt vieler Menschen Sinnen.	Stirs the senses of many a person.
Mein schimmerndes Gewehr	My gleaming armament
Nebst meiner Söhne gleichen Schritten	Alongside my sons' even paces
Und ihre heldenmässge Sitten	And their heroic customs
Vermehren immer mehr und mehr	Increase ever more and more
Des heutgen Tages süsse Freude.	The sweet joy of the present day.

5. *Pallas*: Fromme Musen! meine Glieder!	5. Faithful Muses, members [of] my [coterie],[164]
Singt nicht längst bekannte Lieder!	Do not sing long-known songs.
Dieser Tag sei eure Lust!	Let this day be your delight.
Füllt mit Freuden eure Brust!	Fill your breast with joy;
Werft so Kiel als Schriften nieder!	Cast down both quill and writings
Und erfreut euch dreimal wieder!	And rejoice three times over.

6. *Pallas*: Unsre Königin im Lande,	6. Our Queen in this land,
Die der Himmel zu uns sandte,	Whom heaven sent to us,
Ist der Musen-Trost und Schutz.	Is the Muses' consolation and protection.
Meine Pierinnen[165] wissen,	My Pierians [Muses],
Die in Ehrfurcht ihren Saum noch küssen,	Who yet kiss her hem in reverence,

---

[164] Pallas Athena was associated with the nine Muses, but technically, she was not a member of what was called "das Musenchor" ("the choir of [the nine] Muses," led by Apollo). In line 3 of movement 9, below, Pallas further addresses her coterie members, the choir of Muses, about the manner in which they should sing. That is, the choir of four characters performing this cantata—Irene, Bellona, Pallas, and Fama—are neither literally nor metaphorically members of the choir of Muses. In the cantatas BWV 1162 (formerly Anh. 18) and 207.2 (formerly 207a), however, the expression "Musenchor" does turn up as a metaphor for Bach's own ensembles. BWV 1162 was designed for the reinauguration of the Thomas School in 1732; since schools and universities were sometimes called a "Musensitz" ("seat of the Muses"), it made good sense for the librettist to call Bach's Thomas School choir a "Musenchor" in those works. In Bach's "Hercules" cantata (BWV 213), the closing ensemble aria is in the voice of the "Chor der Musen."

[165] The "Pierinnen" are the Muses, said to have been born in Pieria.

132 TEXTS

Vor ihr stetes Wohlergehn
Dank und Pflicht und Ton stets zu
erhöhn.
Ja, sie wünschen, dass ihr Leben
Möge lange Lust uns geben.

Do know, for her continued welfare,
To continually lift up thanks and duty
and sound.
Yes, they wish that her life
May long give us delight.

7. *Fama*: Kron und Preis gekrönter
Damen,
Königin! mit deinem Namen
Füll ich diesen Kreis der Welt.
Was der Tugend stets gefällt
Und was nur Heldinnen haben,
Sein[167] dir angeborne Gaben.

7. "Crown and praise[166] of crowned
ladies,"
Queen, with your name
I fill this earthly globe.
That which always pleases virtue
And that which only heroines possess
Are gifts innate to you.

8. *Fama*: So dringe in das weite
Erdenrund
Mein von der Königin erfüllter
Mund!
Ihr Ruhm soll bis zum Axen[168]

8. Thus unto the wide earthly orb

May my mouth press forward, filled
with [praise of] the Queen.
Her renown shall flourish as far as
the axes

Des schön gestirnten Himmels
wachsen,
Die Königin der Sachsen und der
Polen
Sei stets des Himmels Schutz
empfohlen.
So stärkt durch sie der Pol

Of beautifully star-bedecked heaven;

May the Queen of the Saxons and of
the Poles
Be ever commended to heaven's
protection.
Thus the pole [of the earthly-heavenly
axes][169] bolsters, by her,

---

[166] "Preis" here is most probably short for "Lobpreis," as it is in the expression "Gott zum Preis und Ehren" ("to the praise and honor of God").

[167] "Sein" (spelled "seyn" in the original sources), as used here, is a regional form of "sind."

[168] "Die Axe" is an archaic spelling of "die Achse" ("the axis"); "zum Axen" is probably a regional form of "zu den Achsen" (plural), not a grammatically confused rendering of "zur Achse" (singular).

[169] The axis implied here is an imaginary straight line around which the earth rotates, and the axes of the heavens were thought to revolve around the extension of this line.

HISTORICALLY INFORMED RENDERING OF LIBRETTOS 133

So vieler Untertanen längst erwünschtes Wohl.	The well-being long desired by so many subjects.
So soll die Königin noch lange bei uns hier verweilen;	Thus shall the Queen long tarry with us here,
Und spät, ach! spät zum Sternen[170] eilen.	And late, ah, late, hasten to the stars.

9. *Irene*: Blühet, ihr Linden in Sachsen, wie Zedern!	9. Blossom, you lindens in Saxony, like cedars.[171]
Bellona: Schallet mit Waffen und Wagen und Rädern!	Make noise with weapons and chariots and wheels.[172]
Pallas: Singet, ihr Musen, mit völligem Klang!	Sing, you Muses,[173] with full clangor.

The "poles" are the top and bottom ends of an axis (e.g., the North and South Poles are the ends of the earthly axis). The idea in the cantata, apparently, is that since the queen's renown will flourish from pole to pole on the linked earthly-heavenly axes, heaven's blessings will be visited upon her Saxon and Polish subjects. "Der Pol" might additionally refer to natives of Poland. ("Der Pol" means "the pole [of an axis]"; "der Pole" means "the [male] Polish person," and poetically clipping its second syllable would yield "der Pol.")

[170] "Zum Sternen" (rather than the plural form "zu den Sternen") is a German equivalent of the aphorism "[per aspera] ad astra" ("through tribulations to the stars").

[171] The "lindens" (or "lime trees") represent the city of Leipzig, whose name means "settlement where the lime trees stand"; the text here (see also the last line in movement 1) draws on Psalm 92:13–15, which in the Luther Bibles of Bach's day reads, "Der Gerechte . . . wird wachsen wie eine Zeder auf Libanon . . . Und wenn sie gleich alt werden, werden sie dennoch blühen, fruchtbar und frisch sein" ("The righteous one will flourish like a cedar on [the mountain range called] Lebanon . . . And even when [the cedars] become old, they will nevertheless blossom, be fruitful and fresh"). By using this language, the poet declares that the city of Leipzig is "righteous."

[172] Bellona, true to her character, uses language of battle; but to speak, even poetically, of making noise with "chariots *and wheels*" (i.e., as if chariots might generate sound apart from the noise of wheels) may seem a bit strange. The quirky language of this line appears to be derived from Ezekiel 23:24, which in Luther Bibles of Bach's day is sometimes given as "Und werden über dich kommen, gerüstet mit Wagen und Rädern" ("And [the enemies] will overcome you, armed with chariots and wheels"), and sometimes as ". . . gerüst mit Wagen und Reutern" (". . . armed with chariots and horsemen"). The precise meaning of the original Hebrew is nearly inscrutable, but the librettist of Cantata 214 seems to be closely familiar with the verse's problems, as the phrase "mit Waffen und Wagen und Rädern" may well be a better approximation of the Hebrew in Ezekiel 23:24 than Luther's. Remarking on the various sounds of attacking forces, including their chariot wheels, Isaiah 5:28–29, in the Luther Bibles of Bach's day, says that "seiner Rossen Hufe sind wie Felsen geachtet, und ihre Wagenräder wie ein Sturmwind; sie brüllen wie Löwen" ("his horses' hooves are taken heed of as [being as hard as] rocks, and their chariot wheels as a windstorm; they roar, as lions").

[173] On the "choir of Muses," see note 164, above.

Fama: Fröhliche Stunden, ihr freudigen Zeiten!	Cheerful hours, you joyous times!
Gönnt uns noch öfters die güldenen Freuden:	Grant us yet again and again the golden joys:
Königin, lebe, ja lebe noch lang![174]	"Long live the Queen, yes live yet long!"

---

[174] The printed libretto appears to attribute the last three lines to Fama, but the typography, with the last line in larger type following the colon in the previous line, suggests that two lines might belong to Fama and the last to all the characters. Bach takes neither of these positions, setting the three last lines for all four voices throughout.

PART IV
JEWS AND JUDAISM

8

On the Jews and Their So-Called Lies in the Fourth Gospel and Bach's *St. John Passion*

Bach's *St. John Passion* was written to serve, at Good Friday vespers in the principal Lutheran churches of eighteenth-century Leipzig, as an extensive meditation (mostly but not exclusively) on the Gospel of John's narrative of the death of Jesus. It was first performed on April 7, 1724. The performance of Part One took place shortly before the pastor's hour-long homily and Part Two shortly afterward.

What the congregation heard was a forty-minute recitation of the Gospel of John's narrative of the death of Jesus (from 18:1 through 19:42, along with a few interpolations of gospel passages from outside of John), surrounded and interspersed with seventy minutes of post-Reformation Lutheran contemplative commentary[1] and reflection.

The story was told in the somewhat archaic prose of Luther's translation of John's gospel. Bach set its narration and the direct speech of individual characters as simple speaking recitatives, and he set its group utterances as highly animated choruses (today often called "turbae," i.e., crowd choruses, even though there is no mention of a crowd in John's Passion narrative).

---

[1] "Commentary" is used here in a colloquial sense (offering meditations on), not in the academic sense (offering scholarly annotations on the text of a literary work).

Bach against Modernity. Michael Marissen, Oxford University Press. © Oxford University Press 2023.
DOI: 10.1093/oso/9780197669495.003.0008

138 JEWS AND JUDAISM

Much of the commentary appeared in the contemporary rhymed and accented verse of eighteenth-century Lutheran poets. Bach set these reflections in the form of emotionally charged solo and choral arias, a type of song within which instrumental ensembles in turn perform episodes with the singers but perform ritornellos (non-verbal refrains) on their own. Music lovers generally focus on these marvelous numbers, and it is not surprising that the few excerpts from the *St. John Passion* included on Bach's Greatest Hits albums take their material from this category alone.

The remaining reflections were made up of the slightly antiquated rhymed and accented poetry of Lutheran hymn writers of the sixteenth and seventeenth centuries. Bach arranged these old texts with their traditional melodies as relatively sedate chorales in four-part harmony for the entire ensemble of singers and instrumentalists. Here was the very sound of the church.

Sin in Bach's *Passion* and the Fourth Gospel

It was of paramount devotional importance for Bach's audiences to receive admonition and comfort in the face of "original sin," the doctrine (in Lutheran understanding) that human nature is in its essence wholly corrupted through the fall of Adam and Eve into sin. Burdened by guilt, and in every respect at fault, humanity has incurred an infinitely crushing debt. The German word "Schuld," employed markedly in Bach's *St. Matthew Passion* and *St. John Passion*, carries all three of these meanings. Only God possesses the power to reconcile humans to himself, and it was for this purpose that Jesus—the Messiah and divine Son of God—died sacrificially, as the Lamb of God on the cross. In the context of Bach's liturgical music, the moral shortcomings and sinful acts of humans are emphatically the byproducts of a root problem, original sin.

The word "sin" crops up only once in the narrative of Bach's *St. John Passion*, at movement 21g, when Jesus says to Pilate, the

ON THE JEWS AND THEIR SO-CALLED LIES   139

Roman procurator interrogating him for possible rabble-rousing, "You would have no power over me, if it were not handed down to you from on high [i.e., from God]; therefore, the one who has handed me over to you, he has the greater sin."

In his writings on John's Passion narrative, Luther, like many interpreters, advised that often in the Bible, the grammatically singular "one" should be understood as connoting a plural.[2] And indeed, the ones who hand Jesus over *to Pilate*, according to John, are "the Jews" and "the chief priests [of the Jews]."

Here it is crucial to bear in mind that Bach conceived his *St. John Passion* with the assumption that listeners would be familiar not only with the evangelist's Passion narrative but also with the rest of the Gospel of John. John 14:6 states that Jesus, sent by God the Father, is "the way and the truth and the life."[3] Indeed, eternal truth and life are leading concepts in John—to "not believe" in their embodiment, Jesus, is a fundamental sin (John 16:9). Accordingly, even though Pilate has been given power by God to judge the purported evildoer Jesus, the procurator does not escape sin, because he is not aligned with the truth and the life via belief in Jesus. On this account, the "greater sin" belongs, however, to "the Jews."

The Fourth Gospel and Judaism

Here we enter into significant scriptural material that has registered as emotionally and interpretively controversial only in recent times.

Who exactly are the ones said by the Gospel of John to be guilty of "greater sin"? The original Greek text evidently does not mean

---

[2] Bach would have at some point encountered this from Luther's *Sermons on the Gospel of John*, as quoted in the commentary on John 19:11 in Calov, *Die heilige Bibel*, V:937. Bach's copy of this Bible (extensively marked with his own annotations) survives and is now housed at Concordia Seminary in St. Louis, Missouri.

[3] Bach set many restatements of this selfsame phrase to gorgeous double-choir music in his motet *Komm, Jesu, komm* (BWV 229).

140   JEWS AND JUDAISM

for its phrase "hoi Ioudaioi" ("the Jews," nowadays sometimes given in translation as "the Judeans" or "the Jewish leaders") to include any active followers of Jesus, whatever their cultic or ethnic backgrounds. John identifies these followers of Jesus as "the believers" nearly one hundred times, as "the disciples" around seventy times, and as "brothers" twice.[4] This gospel never calls active believers in Jesus "Ioudaioi."

The word "Ioudaioi" appears about seventy times in John, referring—almost always negatively—to worshipers of the God of Israel (including native non-Judeans) who did not yet believe, or no longer believed, or simply did not and would not believe in Jesus as God's Messiah and divine Son. In this scheme of things, certainly some people who were back then (and some people who are now) exclusively "Old Testament" worshipers of the God of Israel would then (and will now) come to be believers in Jesus. If such people then persevered (or now persevere) in this belief, however, then they would then (and will now) no longer be, and in a sense never had been, "Jews." And if such people back then in biblical times abandoned (or if they in our time abandon) this belief permanently, then they would no longer be, and in a sense never had been, "believers."

At John 8:44, another key passage, Jesus says to the Jews, in Luther's rendering, "You are of the father the devil, and you want to act according to your father's desire; he is a murderer from the beginning, and is not constituted in the truth, because the truth is not in him; if he speaks lies, then he speaks from his own nature, for he is a liar, and a father of liars."[5] Consider also John 8:40, in which Jesus says to the Jews, "You are seeking to kill me—this person—I

---

[4] Paul Trebilco, *Self-Designations and Group Identity in the New Testament* (Cambridge: Cambridge University Press, 2012), 53–54, 114–117.

[5] Luther Bibles of Bach's day: "Ihr seid von dem Vater dem Teufel, und nach eures Vaters Lust wollt ihr tun; derselbige ist ein Mörder von Anfang, und ist nicht bestanden in der Wahrheit; denn die Wahrheit ist nicht in ihm; wenn er die Lügen redet, so redet er von seinem eigen[en]; denn er ist ein Lügner, und ein Vater derselbigen."

ON THE JEWS AND THEIR SO-CALLED LIES   141

who have said the truth to you."[6] At John 8:55, Jesus reiterates that the Jews are liars; this passage appears within the gospel portion that in Bach's day was read and preached upon every year in the Lutheran churches on the fifth Sunday in Lent, shortly before Good Friday. Then, in John 16:2, Jesus reiterates that the Jews are killers; this passage appears within the portion that was read and preached upon every year on the Sunday after Ascension Day.[7]

Some expositors of the doctrine of original sin famously insist that humans are not sinners because they sin; instead, they sin because humans are sinners by nature, which poisons their volition.[8] By a similar logic, the Gospel of John appears to maintain that Jews are not liars and murderers because they lie and murder; instead, they lie and murder because Jews are by nature (and volition) liars and murderers. As such, the Gospel of John would appear to move well beyond teaching simple disagreement and beyond imparting only prophetic critique—both of which are not ethically troubling—into the teaching of marked contempt, which *is* ethically troubling.[9]

Luther took inspiration from John 8:44 for the title of his infamous screed *On the Jews and Their Lies*, first published in 1543.[10] Bach owned two printings of this treatise.[11]

The most fundamental of Jewish lies, in Luther's reckoning, is that Jesus is neither the Messiah (i.e., God's anointed king) nor the divine

---

[6] Luther Bibles of Bach's day: "Ihr suchet mich zu tödten, einen solchen Menschen, der ich euch die Wahrheit gesagt habe."

[7] The first chorus in Bach's church cantata *Sie werden euch in den Bann tun* (BWV 44) is a powerful setting of this vehement text.

[8] Augustine is the theologian most often associated with this view. Some of the Greek fathers of the church, however, did not hold it.

[9] For a more sanguine view of the Gospel of John and its relation to Bach's works and to modern Judaism, see the section "'Anti-Judaism' and John's Gospel" in Jeremy Begbie, "Bach and Theology," in *Rethinking Bach*, ed. Bettina Varwig (New York: Oxford University Press, 2021), 170–175.

[10] Martin Luther, *Von den Juden und ihren Lügen—Neu bearbeitet und kommentiert von Matthias Morgenstern* (Berlin: Berlin University Press, 2016).

[11] Martin Luther, *Aller Deutschen Bücher und Schrifften* (Altenburg, 1661–1664), VIII:208–274; Martin Luther, *Aller [Deutschen] Bücher und Schrifften* (Jena, 1555–1558; various reprints), VIII:54b–117b (in the reprints, VIII:49a–106a).

142 JEWS AND JUDAISM

Son of God. It is precisely these two so-called fundamental lies of the Jews that come into focus within the narrative at choruses 21f and 23b of Bach's *St. John Passion*. In 21f, "the Jews answered" Pilate that Jesus "*has made himself* God's son" (i.e., they "lie" in proclaiming that Jesus is not the divine Son of God). And in 23b, "the Jews shouted" to Pilate that Jesus "*makes himself* king" (i.e., they "lie" in proclaiming that Jesus is not the Messiah). Choruses 21f and 23b are correspondingly linked by matching musical settings.

These two movements are given further emphasis by the fact that they appear in the middle of a series of eight musically matched biblical chorus settings in the quasi-symmetrical layout A/B, C, D to D, C, A/B. The four choruses 23f/25b and 18b/21b figure at the outer edges of the pattern. Next in from these are choruses 23d and 21d, and choruses 23b and 21f appear in the middle of the series. This sequence of biblical choruses falls entirely within the portion of John's narrative in which Pilate is on the scene in movements 16a through 25c, and it commences right at the moment when Pilate, on the first of three occasions (see 18a, 21c, and 21e), declares to the Jews about Jesus, "I find no fault in him."

Bach's biblical choruses project a ferocity and redoubled insistence that dwarf the settings of previous or contemporary composers. Consider especially the length and relentlessness of 23d, in which "the Jews" are shouting, "Away, away with him; crucify him!" and 21d, in which "the chief priests and the attendants" of the Jews are shouting, "Crucify, crucify!" Bach arguably went far beyond the call of duty in depicting Jewish opposition to Jesus,[12] and he is documented as having conducted this *Passion* a good number

---

[12] For a different view, consider, e.g., how Butt, in his influential book *Bach's Dialogue with Modernity*, 150–151, seeks to validate on dramaturgical (that is, on artistic) grounds his speaking slightingly of hearing the musical settings of the so-called crowd choruses in Bach's *St. John Passion* and *St. Matthew Passion* as specifically anti-Jewish: "In recent years . . . the [great artistic] success that Bach seems to have achieved in setting the words of the crowd [in the Passion narratives from the gospels of John and Matthew] has led some to hear the music as specifically anti-Semitic (insipid music would seemingly have been more acceptable [to these apparently somewhat philistinic listeners]); . . . the text-music relationship is [believed by these listeners to be] clear enough for this music to be

ON THE JEWS AND THEIR SO-CALLED LIES   143

of times in Leipzig from the 1720s through the 1740s. Be that as it may, in its commentary movements, Bach's *St. John Passion* does not meditate either positively or negatively on Jews and Judaism. As far as the commentary and reflections are concerned, the Jews are unobserved and in effect forgotten.

Enlightenment in Leipzig?

One scholar has recently suggested that there appears to have been in the Leipzig of Bach's day a maturing spirit of openness and fairness toward Jews, such that by the 1730s, the times had indeed changed and that it certainly would have been unlikely, for example, to encounter anti-Jewish reflection within the sermons and the choral music delivered in the city's churches.[13]

---

subject to . . . [the] revealing [of] hidden cultural . . . biases of which the [composer] was not necessarily conscious." See also Butt, *Bach's Dialogue with Modernity*, 157–159, an extended authorial "impersonation" (his term; in truth, I would say, a caricature) of anti-Jewish construals of the music in the biblical choruses from Bach's *St. John Passion*; for Butt's partly counterbalancing commentary, however, see 160. It is worth making clear that hearing the music of Bach's *Passions* as specifically anti-Jewish is not just a recent phenomenon, and I would also point out that the contempt for Jews perceived in Bach's music has typically been understood not as a *hidden* but as a *manifest* quality of the work. I would further note that before the end of World War II, any anti-Jewish sentiment that might be sensed in Bach was typically put forward as a *good* thing. For blistering but representative examples among the leading earlier writings on Bach, see Carl Hermann Bitter, *Johann Sebastian Bach* (Berlin: Wilhelm Baensch, 1881), 2:110–114, which argued that, in his *Passion* music, Bach "depicted the Jewish people in its distinctiveness, [a people who are a] potent force which, from wherever it floods unleashed, will respect no bounds and will violate divine and human law with scorn." Bitter went on to say that the "fanaticism" and "terrorism" [*sic*; *Terrorismus*] of Jews "[is musically confronted, however,] in the calm greatness of the chorales, with the ideal community," the church, which is "a becalming contrast against the wildly roaring torrent of Jewry"; indeed, Bitter fundamentally claimed, at 2:90, that "in this basic [Jews-against-Christians] configuration of the [musical] work, one must clearly see the hand of the master, his touch of genius." The classic Bach biographer Philipp Spitta, in *Johann Sebastian Bach* (Leipzig: Breitkopf & Härtel, 1873–1880), 2:357–379, wrote likewise about contempt for Jews in Bach's musical settings as an overt, readily discernible (and *welcome*) thing.

[13] Raymond Erickson, "The Early Enlightenment, Jews, and Bach: Further Considerations," *Understanding Bach* 9 (2014): 97; see also Raymond Erickson, "The Early Enlightenment, Jews, and Bach," *Musical Quarterly* 94 (2011): 518–547.

144 JEWS AND JUDAISM

But a still little-noticed discovery had already created at least some inconvenience for this incompletely established picture of across-the-board progress toward "modernity" in Leipzig. A copy of the printed libretto booklets that were made available to the congregants of the Thomaskirche in Leipzig for the 1734 Good Friday *Passion* performance surfaced more than ten years ago in Russia, of all places.[14] Gottfried Heinrich Stölzel, Kapellmeister at the court in Gotha (about a hundred miles from Leipzig), wrote the text and the music for this work, entitled "Ein Lämmlein geht und trägt die Schuld." His commentary expresses anti-Jewish sentiment that is a good deal more contemptuous than anything encountered in music known to have been performed in the Leipzig churches in earlier times.

At the eighth meditation in Stölzel's work, for example, the Believing Soul sings, upon Pilate's declaring Jesus to be innocent: "Hear, *damned Jew*, what a *Gentile/heathen* says here. . . . If you won't have him [Jesus] as King, then he [Jesus] will one day be your stern judge; if his eternal kingdom should not nurture you, *then just go on to hell*."[15]

Conclusions

For whatever reason, the commentary movements in Bach's *Passion*, unlike in Stölzel's, communicate no interest in the supposed perfidy

[14] Tatjana Shabalina, "'Texte zur Music' in Sankt Petersburg: Neue Quellen zur Leipziger Musikgeschichte sowie zur Kompositions- und Aufführungstätigkeit Johann Sebastian Bachs," *Bach-Jahrbuch* 94 (2008): 33–98.

[15] Stölzel: "*Verdammter Jüde* hör, was hier ein *Heide* spricht. / . . . Willst du ihm nicht zum König haben, / So wird er einst dein strenger Richter sein; / Soll dich sein ewges Reich nicht laben, / *So geh nur in die Höll hinein*." This movement's title is listed as "Verdammter Jüde hör" in Shabalina, "Texte zur Music in Sankt Petersburg: Neue Quellen," 81. Significantly contemptuous anti-Jewish reflection was apparently delivered again in the very next year's Good Friday music through a performance of Georg Philipp Telemann's Passion oratorio *Seliges Erwägen*; evidence for a 1735 liturgical rendering of this work at Leipzig's Nikolaikirche is provided in Christine Blanken, Christoph Wolff, and Peter Wollny, *Bach-Werke-Verzeichnis (BWV): Thematisch-systematisches Verzeichnis der musikalischen Werke von Johann Sebastian Bach*, 3rd ed. (Wiesbaden: Breitkopf & Härtel, 2022), xiii, 661.

of the Jews. When all is said and done, the transgressors held most pointedly accountable for Jesus's crucifixion in the *St. John Passion*'s reflections are Bach's intended Christian audiences.

The hymn meditating on Jesus being struck in the face by one of the attendants of the Jews—movement 11—expresses matters the most forcibly, its "I" referring to Bach's fellow Lutheran congregants: "Who has struck you so? . . . I, I and my sins, which are as numerous as the grains of sand on the seashore; they have caused you the sorrow that strikes you and the grievous host of pain."

Such commentary may be a historically unexpected and welcome palliative, but surely it would be ethically careless to suppose that it erases any and all qualms about contemptuous anti-Judaism in Bach's work. One hopes very much against hope that a heightened awareness of and attentiveness to Bach's setting will give scope for seeing, in the words of the great rabbinics scholar Jacob Neusner, "the *St. John Passion* as occasion to identify and overcome anti-Judaism and anti-Semitism—a work of aesthetic refinement and deep religious sentiment."[16]

---

[16] Neusner's comment appeared within his long blurb for the dust jacket of Michael Marissen, *Lutheranism, Anti-Judaism, and Bach's* St. John Passion (New York: Oxford University Press, 1998).

9

Bach and Sons in the Jewish Salon Culture of Nineteenth-Century Berlin

In 1788, the last year of his life, Carl Philipp Emanuel Bach, director of church music in Hamburg, composed a Double Concerto in E-flat that calls—somewhat remarkably—for harpsichord and piano as the two soloists.[1]

By that time, on the eve of the French Revolution, the relatively novel and forward-looking piano had only just recently displaced the not-far-from-old-fangled harpsichord as secular music's reigning keyboard instrument.

Late-eighteenth-century pianos looked very much like harpsichords, but the two instruments did not sound alike. The piano's timbre (tone color) differed from the harpsichord's in the same way that the intrinsic sound of a flute differs from the sound of a recorder. Furthermore, whereas a harpsichord will not sound any louder if its keys are pressed harder, the loudness of a piano is entirely determined by how hard its keys are struck. Not surprisingly, composers had come by the 1780s to write keyboard music in a new manner that was idiomatically expressive and fitting for the piano, music that would not always "work" successfully on the harpsichord.

---

[1] For a magnificent recording, listen to tracks 10–12 of the album *Carl Philipp Emanuel Bach: Concerti*, Freiburger Barockorchester (Carus, 2005).

Bach against Modernity. Michael Marissen, Oxford University Press. © Oxford University Press 2023.
DOI: 10.1093/oso/9780197669495.003.0009

By the late eighteenth century, it was unusual for a composer to devise, as C. P. E. Bach had done, an orchestral concerto specifying harpsichord and piano as the soloists but featuring completely undifferentiated keyboard writing. That is to say, in this piece, neither solo part attends to the distinctive musical features of the particular keyboard instrument that the composer, for some reason, went to the pains of specifically designating.

C. P. E. Bach's double concerto was apparently commissioned by the German Jewish *salonnière* Sara Itzig Levy of Berlin, a virtuoso keyboard recitalist (an unusual line of endeavor for a woman, Jewish or Gentile, at the time), who very likely asked that the piece be composed specifically for harpsichord and piano as radical equals.

Levy was a daughter of Daniel Itzig, who had become a fabulously wealthy "court Jew" even though his father had been a mere horse trader. On account of his extraordinary services to the Prussian monarchy, Itzig was rewarded with citizenship for his family, down to the third generation. (That is, they were granted an exception to the legal requirement for citizenship of actually or nominally converting to Christianity; thus, for example, the children of Itzig's granddaughter Lea Salomon and her husband Abraham Mendelssohn—most notably, Felix Mendelssohn and Fanny Hensel—were able, as fourth-generation descendants, to obtain citizenship only by dint of Christian baptism.)

The Itzigs collected valuable music manuscripts and put on sophisticated house concerts, fixing so intently on the music of C. P. E. Bach and his father, Johann Sebastian Bach, that the Itzigs were said to be devoted to "a downright cult of Sebastian and Philipp Emanuel Bach."[2] From the 1780s, Sara Itzig Levy likewise devoted herself to manuscript collecting and to hosting salons centered

---

[2] For the background, see Peter Wollny, *"Ein förmlicher Sebastian und Philipp Emanuel Bach-Kultus": Sara Levy und ihr musikalisches Wirken* (Wiesbaden: Breitkopf & Härtel, 2010).

148 JEWS AND JUDAISM

largely on music, especially the music of J. S. Bach and his sons. She was a formidable performer on both harpsichord and piano and had been the only student, it seems, of Wilhelm Friedemann Bach (C. P. E. Bach's older brother) during his time in Berlin. Her husband, the banker Samuel Salomon Levy, was evidently a quite proficient flute player.

At Levy's salons, men and women, Jews and Christians, aristocrats and bourgeois, all gathered to drink tea and eat finger food; engage in convivial conversation about literature, art, philosophy, and politics; and hear performances of certain old-fashioned and newer repertories of instrumental music whose styles we now call high baroque and pre-classical. The programs consisted mostly of orchestral, chamber, and keyboard music in the forms of concertos, fantasias, preludes and fugues, and sonatas. Levy's salons cultivated serious but somewhat "abstract" types of music, repertory that as a rule was without emphatic religious, social-class, or gendered associations. Such intellectually satisfying and emotionally sanguine art must have seemed perfectly fitting and appealing in the context of the optimistic Enlightenment ideals of the Jews and Christians who attended her events, including such luminaries as Gustav Droysen, Johann Gottlieb Fichte, Henriette Herz, Alexander and Wilhelm von Humboldt, Friedrich Schleiermacher, Rahel Varnhagen, and many others. An earnest ethical aspect of the inspiration behind Levy's salons was that even the so-called purely aesthetic experience of jointly hearing these types of music was thought to help its disparate listeners become more empathetic persons.

Which brings us back to C. P. E. Bach's double concerto. This piece looks to be tailor-made for the Enlightenment milieu of Levy's salons. Manifold topics of pleasant musical "conversation" develop in each of the concerto's three movements. Moods vary subtly or dramatically from one utterance to the next. Individual instruments even politely finish one another's phrases. In addition, the concerto's finale is an emphatically upbeat contredanse, whose

BACH AND SONS IN THE JEWISH SALON CULTURE   149

main theme appears at the codetta with staggered overlapping entries at normal, half, and quarter speeds[3]—a wonderful and riotously joyous evocation of what philosophers might call "the supratemporal sublime."

This double concerto, throughout, is such an extreme example of unity in variety that one has to wonder if there were not special extramusical factors that contributed to its genesis. The famous German Jewish Enlightenment thinker Moses Mendelssohn, a figure admired by Jews and Christians then and now, had argued that in society (as in art), what ought to be valued is unity in variety. Indeed, in this view, Jews should without question be granted full citizenship, because society can only benefit from an integrated citizenry that is built up of fundamental religious diversity. Christianity must never be allowed to supplant Judaism, and general Enlightenment thought and practice must never be allowed to "erase" Judaism. What are we to make, then, of the fact that the original manuscript of C. P. E. Bach's double concerto was wrapped in a folder on which the title of the work appears in Levy's handwriting and on which, in the upper corner, Carl Friedrich Zelter, a leading light in Berlin musical circles (he was the director of the Berlin Singakademie and also of an associated instrumental ensemble that Levy occasionally performed with as a keyboard soloist), has scrawled, "From Madam Levy, as a gift, on 8 October 1813"? Surely it is rather suggestive for our topic that this date in the Gregorian calendar was 14 Tishrei 5574—Erev Sukkot—in the Jewish calendar.

Levy was a prominent member of the Jewish community in Berlin, and she could hardly have been unaware that October 8, 1813, fell on the day before Sukkot, the Feast of Booths. Given that Zechariah 14:1–21 is the Haftarah in the liturgy for the first day of Sukkot, Levy presumably would have known, further, that according to verse 16 of the Haftarah portion, this most joyous of

---

[3] At 3:49–3:58 in track 12 of the album listed in note 1, above.

150   JEWS AND JUDAISM

annual Jewish festivals would, in a prophesied ideal future, mark the occasion of an ingathering of the Gentiles to Jerusalem "to worship the King YHWH of Hosts." What a lovely metaphorical way, then, to celebrate a notion of biblically prophesied ideal Jewish-with-Gentile worship of God, namely, by bestowing upon a non-Jewish musical colleague the autograph score of a marvelous double concerto that exuberantly brings together into complete musical unity its separate-but-equally-treated keyboard instruments, a pair that might reasonably have been expected in the late 1780s to be compositionally at odds on account of their differing sonance and relative "standing."

Much of the music known to have been owned by Levy has been performed in recent decades, in concerts and on commercial recordings, but mixed in with other high baroque and preclassical repertory, typically without any awareness of the music's connections with Levy's library and her salons.[4]

Only recently have musicians zeroed in on the Levy repository of musical manuscripts as such, with the aim of taking stock of Levy and her music's cultural and historical significance.

At the forefront of this effort is the brilliant music historian and gifted keyboard player Rebecca Cypess, a music professor at Rutgers University. She and her musician colleagues the Raritan Players have produced a superb album titled *In Sara Levy's Salon* (Acis Productions, 2017),[5] which, for readily understandable practical reasons, explores selections not from the relatively large-ensemble music in the Levy orbit but rather from the smaller-scale chamber music, in this case for various configurations of cello, flute, fortepiano, harpsichord, viola, and violin.

The program for Cypess's album was extremely well chosen, both from a musical and from a historical-cultural point of view. There

---

[4] The most convenient way to get a substantial idea of the musical contents from the Levy collection is to visit http://www.rism.info/home/ and search for "Sara Levy."

[5] This chapter was originally a review essay about the recording.

BACH AND SONS IN THE JEWISH SALON CULTURE 151

are seven works altogether, arranged such that one moves from one genre to the next in this way: Quartet–Solo–Trio–Solo–Trio–Solo–Quartet. This symmetrical layout has the effect, even if only subliminally, of imposing an overarching unity upon the striking stylistic variety of the program's constituent parts.

The works performed are:

- Quartet in E minor for Flute and Strings, QV 4:9, by Johann Joachim Quantz.
- Sonata in G major for Keyboard, Wq. 56/II, by C. P. E. Bach—here played on piano.
- Trio in C minor for Two Harpsichords, BWV 526, by J. S. Bach—here played on piano with harpsichord.
- Andante in E minor for Keyboard, Fk. 40/ii, by W. F. Bach—here played on piano.
- Trio in E-flat major for Flute, Violin, and Continuo, BWV 1031, by J. S. [?] Bach.
- Variations on "God Save the King" for Clavichord or Piano, by Johann Nikolaus Forkel—here played on piano.
- Quartet in D major for Flute, Viola, and Keyboard, Wq. 94, by C. P. E. Bach—here with the keyboard part played on piano.

Fittingly, at the center of the program is a delicately brooding slow movement composed by Bach the son, Wilhelm Friedemann, Levy's beloved teacher. On either side are signally contrasting trios by Bach the father.

In truth, there has been a good deal of scholarly debate about who was the composer of the lovely Trio in E-flat major for Flute, Violin, and Continuo (BWV 1031), as its easygoing style—with upper voices for flute and violin that either continually move in pleasant dialogue or amble along in tandem, accompanied by an almost entirely non-thematic bass line—is difficult to reconcile with the rest of J. S. Bach's typically much more exacting output, where all the voices are melodic in character. (Even Levy's manuscript

152 JEWS AND JUDAISM

copy of this trio was at first labeled simply "Dal Sigre Bach" ["By Herr Bach"] and only later expanded to read "Dal Sigre Giov. Seb. Bach" ["By Herr Johann Sebastian Bach"].)

The Trio in C minor for Two Harpsichords (BWV 526), on the other hand, is baroque music of the highest order. Over the past nearly half-century, I have heard the piece countless times in its familiar version for solo organ, but I do not mind admitting that I wept the first time I heard this exquisite and touching rendition with Cypess on harpsichord and Yi-heng Yang on fortepiano. What must the Berlin salon guests have thought and felt when they were treated to performances of this staggering keyboard duet? Here a limited number of strongly asserted ideas are relentlessly stated, restated, texturally inverted, explored, expounded, hammered, and re-hammered. What one encounters is really not so much a dialogue as a monologue—more akin in style and structure to an old-school Protestant sermon than a reasoned dialectical argument that ultimately resolves.

The remaining pieces on Cypess's program are once again, then, much more straightforwardly "conversational" in style and structure.

Particularly rewarding to listen to are the Sonata in G major for Keyboard and the Quartet in D major for Flute, Viola, and Keyboard by C. P. E. Bach. The closing quartet appears to have been commissioned by Levy, and, just as with the Double Concerto in E-flat, it was written in the last year of the composer's life and features keenly Enlightened musical dialogue that sounds tailor-made for Levy's salon.

The Quartet in E minor for Flute and Strings by Johann Joachim Quantz, on the other hand, provides extremely satisfying and solid high baroque repertory to open the entire program.

Most will agree that Johann Nikolaus Forkel's set of Variations on "God Save the King" for Clavichord or Piano is a tedious work (it was also severely criticized in its own day), and Cypess mercifully has chosen to perform only ten of the twenty-four variations—hers is clearly a generous soul, though, in view of the fact that she does manage occasionally to find some poetry in this unpromising material.[6] I would guess that Cypess the music historian just could not resist including this marginal work from Levy's music collection: its composer is now celebrated for having been one of the founders of the field of musicology, and he was the author of the first scholarly monograph on J. S. Bach, published in 1802 with the rather outré title "Über Johann Sebastian Bachs Leben, Kunst und Kunstwerke—Für patriotische Verehrer echter musikalischer Kunst" ("On Johann Sebastian Bach's Life, Art, and Artworks—For Patriotic Honorers of True Musical Art").

Listening to recorded albums is, of course, quite different from experiencing live recitals in a concert hall or a salon music room. At first, I was taken aback by the very brief pauses between the seven works on this album, but then I quickly came to feel that this was in truth the perfect approach for this recording (was it consciously intended by the performers?). The effect of having these only very brief breaks between works is to place the varying works themselves still more powerfully into dialogue with one another than was already brought about by the symmetrical "architecture" of the entire program.

Rarely do albums of classical music provide such great insight into cultural history at the same time that they give such intense aesthetic pleasure. I hope and expect that this terrific project will stimulate further research on Levy, a fascinating but still, alas, somewhat elusive figure.[7]

---

[6] Especially true for variation 23, which is at 7:51–10:20 in track 14 on the album.

[7] In the meantime, readers will also want to consult the six pages of excellent liner notes by Cypess that come with the hard copy of the album under review; and, moreover, they will certainly want to consult the various essays in Rebecca Cypess and Nancy Sinkoff, eds., *Sara Levy's World: Gender, Judaism, and the Bach Tradition in Enlightenment Berlin* (Rochester, NY: University of Rochester Press, 2018). Another album of Berlin salon repertory well worth listening to is *Johann Gottlieb Janitsch: Rediscoveries from the Sara Levy Collection*, by Tempesta di Mare: Philadelphia Baroque Orchestra (Chandos Records, 2018). I might add that Levy and her milieu are also brought to life fictionally in Lauren Belfer, *And After the Fire: A Novel* (New York: Harper, 2016). (Full disclosure: Belfer is my spouse.)

PART V

THEOLOGICAL CHARACTER OF SECULAR INSTRUMENTAL MUSIC

10

Bach's Sacred *Brandenburg Concertos*

One of the most persistent myths about Bach is that his work is marked by a fundamental conflict between the sacred and the secular.[1]

According to this view, Bach's ideal appointment was his stint from 1717 to '23 as Kapellmeister (director of music) for Prince Leopold of Anhalt-Köthen. Leopold's court observed the Calvinist faith, a liturgically austere branch of Protestantism that prohibited elaborate music in its church services.

So here—unlike in his previous positions at the Lutheran court of Weimar and at Lutheran parishes in Arnstadt and Mühlhausen— Bach was freed from having to continually oblige the church. He could focus instead on "pure" instrumental music, like the "Brandenburg" Concertos, today's holiday-season standbys.

But was that truly his goal? Listeners and scholars who speak of Bach's works as "sacred" versus "secular" generally understand these terms to mean "religious" as opposed to "nonreligious."[2] Bach and most of his contemporaries, however, don't seem to have understood sacred and secular to be mutually exclusive categories. The distinction they observed was between liturgical music (for the church service) and secular music (out in the world).

---

[1] The main text of this chapter reproduces verbatim the wording of this essay as it appeared in the *New York Times*, which licenses permission to reprint its text but not to revise it. I will thus include a few informational footnotes to accommodate differences in style from the rest of this book and provide a few clarifying notes.

[2] That is, they understand the term "secular" in a modern, anachronistic way, namely, to mean "not having to do with God," as if in Bach's world, the word "secular" was synonymous with "secularist."

Bach against Modernity. Michael Marissen, Oxford University Press. © Oxford University Press 2023.
DOI: 10.1093/oso/9780197669495.003.0010

158 THEOLOGICAL CHARACTER OF SECULAR MUSIC

Secular and liturgical works were *both* religious: A central purpose of all serious-minded music, wherever performed, was to honor God.[3] Consider Bach's manuscripts for the Six Harpsichord Concertos (BWV 1052–57) and the church cantata "Now come, savior of the gentiles" (BWV 62),[4] both of which open with his inscription "Jesus, help me" right before the first bar of music and close with "To God alone the glory" after the last bar.

Those today who view religion negatively sometimes go even further and view Bach's church cantatas as essentially instrumental concertos,[5] with the religious texts more or less extraneous. But historically informed interpretation suggests the opposite: Bach's *instrumental* concertos, including the "Brandenburgs," are essentially church cantatas with implicit (and therefore harder-to-read) "texts" that do have real meaning.[6]

In the 1721 presentation manuscript that he dedicated (probably as a veiled job query) to "His Royal Highness: Monseigneur Christian Ludwig, Margrave of Brandenburg & So Forth," Bach had called this collection "Six Concertos with Various Instruments." The name "Brandenburg" Concertos was coined in the 19th century by the leading Bach biographer Philipp Spitta. (We can be grateful that Bach and Spitta were unaware that Ludwig's true primary title was Margrave of Schwedt: The "Schwedt" Concertos doesn't have much of a ring to it.)

Scholarly consensus now holds that Bach composed some of the "Brandenburg" Concertos during his Köthen tenure and others in his final years at Weimar. But although his aristocratic employers, had they known about it, might have disapproved of his formally

---

[3] That is, to express this in a more nuanced fashion, secular and liturgical works *both had to do with God*, given that a central purpose—in addition to offering human pleasure and refreshment—of all serious-minded music, wherever performed, was to honor God.

[4] *Nun komm, der Heiden Heiland* (BWV 62).

[5] That is, as essentially *secularist* instrumental concertos.

[6] That is, to express this in a more nuanced fashion, the *Brandenburg Concertos* may be thought of as essentially godly works—differing in degree, but not kind, from Bach's church cantatas—with designs that *do* project theological meaning.

BACH'S SACRED *BRANDENBURG CONCERTOS*   159

dedicating any of "their" music to someone else, it hardly seems likely that in 1721 Bach could have drawn upon an untapped hoard of concertos.

So by all indications, the "Brandenburgs" would have been included in the weekly programs of the Köthen palace concerts, and these pieces do indeed line up well with Leopold's documented interests. Remarkably, the prince's investiture festivities, in 1716, had included not only a superabundance of concert offerings, but also a scholarly oration exploring how musical order and societal order are analogous.[7]

As it happens, each of the six "Brandenburgs" delves into issues of hierarchy and order. The Sixth is musically and socially the most unconventional of the set. Two violas, with cello, are pitted against two viols, with violone.

At the time, violas were customarily low-rent, undemanding orchestral instruments, while viols were high-end, virtuoso solo instruments. Bach reversed these roles, such that the violas perform virtuosic solo lines while the viols amble along in repeated eighth notes. Pursuing these two radical instrumental treatments within the same work was unprecedented (and wouldn't be imitated).

It's an excellent musical illustration of the time-honored theme of the "world upside down." Visual examples include mice chasing cats; servants riding on horseback while noblemen have to go behind on foot; and peasants serving communion in the cathedral while priests sweep the adjacent streets.

These kinds of inversions play a significant part in Christian scripture, which frequently proclaims that with God the first shall be last while the last shall be first; the lowly shall be exalted while the exalted shall be brought low.

The function of the world upside down imagery in Bach's Lutheranism, as in scripture, was not to foment earthly upheaval,

---

[7] Günter Hoppe, "Köthener politische, ökonomische und höfische Verhältnisse als Schaffensbedingungen Bachs (Teil 1)," *Cöthener Bach-Hefte* 4 (1986): 30–31.

160 THEOLOGICAL CHARACTER OF SECULAR MUSIC

but to inspire heavenly comfort: The hierarchies of this sinful world are a necessary injustice for the sake of order, but, in light of the equality that awaits the blessed in paradise, they are ephemeral.

A marvelous example of inverted imagery in Bach's church cantatas is the fourth movement of "Whoever lets only the dear God rule" (BWV 93),[8] where a soprano-alto duet gives voice to a hymn text by means of instrument-like countermelodies, while the violins and viola nonverbally intone the actual hymn tune. Voices and instruments, upside down.

All three movements of the Fourth "Brandenburg" feature a solo violin part that is continually overshadowed by a duo of lowly recorders. Today's listeners revel in the violin's isolated flurry of activity about three minutes into the first movement.

The audiences at Leopold's palace, however, would have heard this as an egregious breach of musical and social decorum. The violin's rowdy flare-up occurs not within an episodic solo section, as it ought properly to have done, but interloping into the start of the group refrain, an elegant French court dance led by the pair of recorders.

A parallel example of a soloist's hollow virtuosity fluttering atop an elegant dance-like group refrain is the alto aria from Bach's church cantata "Whoever may love me will keep my word" (BWV 74).[9] Here the violin's jangling figurations serve to bolster the text's notion that Jesus's blood renders the enraged rattling of hell's chains as comically useless.

In the first movement from the Fifth "Brandenburg," the three soloists—flute, violin and harpsichord—work episode-by-episode to undercut the sway of the ensemble refrain, set in the "stile concitato" (the militant style, projected by repeated 16th notes).

At their second episode, the flute and violin take up bits of the group refrain's pitch content, but reconfigure it in the "stile

---

[8] *Wer nur den lieben Gott lässt walten* (BWV 93).
[9] *Wer mich liebet, der wird mein Wort halten* (BWV 74).

BACH'S SACRED *BRANDENBURG CONCERTOS*   161

affettuoso" (tender style, here projected by smoothly connected pairs of eighth notes).

It's only a few steps from there before the harpsichord—in pre-1721 concertos, conventionally just a humble chordal-accompaniment instrument—assumes an ever more unruly star-soloist character and completely overwhelms the ensemble.

The most powerful example in Bach of undermining the "stile concitato" by "stile affettuoso" occurs in the aria for bass and chorus from his church cantata "Hold Jesus Christ in remembrance" (BWV 67),[10] where Satan the violence-bringer is stunningly subdued by Jesus the peace-bringer.

In the egalitarian treatment of his eccentric combination of soloists for the Second "Brandenburg," Bach abandoned altogether the hierarchies of his "various instruments." Here the high-and-mighty trumpet, lofty solo violin, middling oboe and lowly recorder uncharacteristically perform interchangeable lines of undifferentiated passagework.

A similar leveling of the Baroque orchestra can be found in the interchangeable writing for trumpets, strings, oboes and recorders in the choruses from the cantata "Jerusalem, praise the Lord" (BWV 119).[11]

The fluidity between the secular and liturgical in Bach is also illustrated by the fact that several Brandenburg Concertos find repurposing in his church cantatas for Leipzig, where he moved after Köthen. Bach employed the first movement from the First "Brandenburg"—doubtless on account of its riotously flamboyant horn parts—as the Sinfonia for "False world, I do not trust you" (BWV 52);[12] and he arranged a souped-up version of the first movement from the Third Concerto—with its triadic trinity of

---

[10] *Halt im Gedächtnis Jesum Christ* (BWV 67).
[11] *Preise, Jerusalem, den Herrn* (BWV 119).
[12] *Falsche Welt, dir trau ich nicht* (BWV 52).

162 THEOLOGICAL CHARACTER OF SECULAR MUSIC

three violins, three violas and three cellos—as the Sinfonia for "I love [God] the most high with all my mind" (BWV 174).[13]

Accepting the idea that the "Brandenburg" Concertos harbor social and religious designs needn't involve downplaying the magnificence of Bach's artistic gifts. But insisting on exclusively aesthetic contemplation of his works—or implying that in the "Brandenburgs" he was freed from the perceived burden of including religious content in his music—pales their meanings, diminishes their complexity and reduces their stature.[14]

[13] *Ich liebe den Höchsten von ganzem Gemüte* (BWV 174).
[14] For a full discussion, see Marissen, *The Social and Religious Designs*.

11

The Serious Nature of the Quodlibet in Bach's *Goldberg Variations*

If there is one thing music lovers "know" about the *Goldberg Variations*, it is the continually trotted-out fun fact that in the final variation, titled "Quodlibet," Bach superimposed the melodies of two merry old German folk songs, "Ich bin so lang nicht bey dir g'west" ("For so Long I Have Not Been with You") and "Kraut und Rüben haben mich vertrieben" ("Cabbage and Turnips Have Driven Me Away").

Scholars and enthusiasts have long found this knowledge attractive, for various reasons. Nationalists fixed on the "old German" element. Communists embraced the "folk" element. Most others focused simply on the "merry."

In his book *Music Comes out of Silence*, renowned Bach interpreter András Schiff fervently backs the merry view: "As the title suggests, [Bach's Quodlibet is] boisterous and very funny. . . . We can imagine the Bach family singing it together with a glass of wine (or was it beer?) in their hands. This is Dionysian music."[1] In an interview for the *Guardian*, he had added: "The [humorous] character of [Bach's Quodlibet] is formed by two folk tunes that would have been easily recognizable to Bach's contemporaries."[2] How

---

[1] András Schiff, *Music Comes out of Silence* (London: Weidenfeld & Nicolson, 2020), 156.

[2] Martin Kettle, "Bach at His Best: The Goldberg Variations Are the Pinnacle of Achievement on the Piano—András Schiff Gives Martin Kettle a Guided Tour," *Guardian*, October 3, 2003, https://www.theguardian.com/arts/fridayreview/story/0,12102,1054166,00.html.

Bach against Modernity. Michael Marissen, Oxford University Press. © Oxford University Press 2023.
DOI: 10.1093/oso/9780197669495.003.0011

164 THEOLOGICAL CHARACTER OF SECULAR MUSIC

plausible is this? In Schiff's hands, the Quodlibet certainly projects greater exuberance than in anyone else's,[3] but to my ears, not even his phenomenal technique and artistry have rendered this music "very funny."

A musical quodlibet was a piece in which well-known tunes appeared either one after another or at the same time. "Successive quodlibets" did tend to be jocular, but "simultaneous quodlibets" could be serious, even melancholy. *Was sind das für grosse Schlösser* (BWV 524), a secular work whose attribution to Bach has generally been accepted by scholars, provides a good example of the successive quodlibet. Melodic snippets from folk songs appear throughout,[4] and musical and verbal jokes abound. Bach's church cantata *Herr Jesu Christ, wahr Mensch und Gott* (BWV 127) provides a good example of the simultaneous quodlibet. Three Lutheran hymn snippets appear in two combinations within the orchestral refrain of the opening movement.[5] The title hymn tune is superimposed initially on "Christe, du Lamm Gottes, der du trägst die Sünd der Welt" ("Christ, You Lamb of God, You Who Bear the Sin of the World") and then on a slightly fuzzy version of what is either "Herzlich tut mich verlangen" ("With My Heart[6] I Long for a Blessed End [in Heaven]") or "O Haupt voll Blut und Wunden" ("O Head Full of Blood and Wounds"). This is one very unfunny quodlibet.

So why is the simultaneous quodlibet from the *Goldberg Variations* supposed to be humorous? The persistently reiterated

---

[3] András Schiff, piano, Goldberg Variations J. S. Bach (ECM Records, 2003).

[4] Details in Günther Kraft, "Zur Entstehungsgeschichte des 'Hochzeitsquodlibet' (BWV 524)," *Bach-Jahrbuch* 43 (1956): 140–154. See also the secular cantata *He! kühne, mé Tate!* (BWV deest).

[5] Michael Praetorius, *Syntagma Musicum III*, ed. and trans. Jeffery T. Kite-Powell (New York: Oxford University Press, 2004; orig. 1618–1619), Part I, Chapter V, "Concerning Compositions Put Together out of Diverse Pieces, Such as the Messanza and the Quodlibet," 33–34, gives only Lutheran chorales as its specifically identified musical examples for inclusion in quodlibets.

[6] "Herzlich" usually means "sincerely" or "heartily," but here it is used in the sense of "with my heart" (i.e., what I feel, inwardly), as typically opposed to "mündlich" in the sense of "with my mouth" (i.e., what I say, outwardly).

THE SERIOUS NATURE OF QUODLIBET   165

"fact" that Bach combined two folk songs—humorous or not—in the *Goldbergs* goes back to a single, uncorroborated source. In the early nineteenth century, Casper Siegfried Gähler, a lawyer, politician, and collector, scribbled into his *Goldbergs* print:

> Aus einer mündlichen Nachricht des berühmten Organisten Johann Christian Kittel, einem Schüler Joh. Seb. Bachs.
>
> In dem letzten Quodlibet sind von zweyen ehemaligen Volksgesängen: Ich bin so lange nicht bey dir gewesen, Rück her, Rück her etc. und Kraut und Rüben haben mich vertrieben etc. die Melodien in eine künstreiche[7] harmonische Verbindung gebracht.
>
> From an oral account [given to me in c. 1801] by the famous organist Johann Christian Kittel, a student [in 1748–1750] of Joh. Seb. Bach.
>
> In the final Quodlibet the melodies of two folk songs from former times—"For so Long I Have Not Been with You, Come Closer, Come Closer" etc., and "Cabbage and Turnips Have Driven Me Away" etc.—are brought into an ingenious concordant combination.[8]

Gähler's copy of the *Goldbergs* later went to the Royal Library in Berlin, and its music librarian, Siegfried Wilhelm Dehn, eventually jotted down the song texts more completely, just below Gähler's note:

> Ich bin so lang nicht bey dir g'west
> Ruck her " — " — "

---

[7] This has sometimes been mistranscribed as "künstliche" ("artful" or "artificial").

[8] This is a transcription of the facsimile of Gähler's note provided in Ingrid Kaussler and Helmut Kaussler, *Die Goldberg-Variationen von J. S. Bach* (Stuttgart: Verlag Freies Geistesleben, 1985), 224. Gähler's copy of the *Goldbergs* print is now held at the British Library, London, Hirsch Collection III.40. See also the transcription of Gähler's note in Hans-Joachim Schulze, ed., *Bach-Dokumente V* (Kassel: Bärenreiter, 2007), 263.

166 THEOLOGICAL CHARACTER OF SECULAR MUSIC

Mit einem [s]tumpfen Flederwisch
drüb'r her, drüb'r her drüb'r her.

&

Kraut u. Rüben haben mich vertrieben
Hätt' meine Mutter Fleisch gekocht
Wär' ich länger g'blieben./blieben.
For so long I have not been with you,
Come closer, come closer, come closer;
With a run-down feather duster,[9]
Over here, over here, over here.

&

Cabbage and turnips have driven me away;
If my mother had cooked meat,
I would have stayed longer.

In his little-known book on comic opera (1774),[10] Johann Friedrich Reichardt had described Bach family gatherings in which humorous quodlibets were sung. Johann Nikolaus Forkel, in his often-quoted Bach biography (1802),[11] supplied the extra detail that these quodlibets were made up of folk songs. Reichardt does not mention the *Goldbergs* Quodlibet. Forkel does, but he says nothing about folk songs or humor. Link parts of Gähler's and Forkel's data together, however, and you can scare up the idea that Bach designed his *Goldberg Variations* to culminate in a jokey quodlibet.

A 1934 essay by the philosopher Otto Baensch,[12] whose interpretation is now widely parroted but rarely attributed, dove more

---

[9] "Flederwisch" ("feather duster") was slang in Bach's day for a maiden who constantly rejects suitors as a matter of course.

[10] Johann Friedrich Reichardt, *Über die Deutsche comische Oper* (Hamburg, 1774), 4; quoted in Hans-Joachim Schulze, "Notizen zu Bachs Quodlibets," in *Bach-Facetten: Essays—Studien—Miszellen*, by Hans-Joachim Schulze (Leipzig: Evangelische Verlagsanstalt, 2017), 164–165.

[11] Johann Nikolaus Forkel, *Über Johann Sebastian Bachs Leben, Kunst und Kunstwerke—Für patriotische Verehrer echter musikalischer Kunst* (Leipzig, 1802), 3–4.

[12] Otto Baensch, "Nochmals das Quodlibet der Goldbergvariationen," *Zeitschrift für Musik* 101 (1934): 322–323.

THE SERIOUS NATURE OF QUODLIBET   167

deeply into this ostensible merriment. The twenty-nine variations preceding the Quodlibet, Baensch proposed, are the "cabbage and turnips" of the second folk song, which have "driven away" the "I" of the first folk song; and the soprano line of the *Goldbergs'* opening movement, titled "Aria," is this "I" who comes back right after the Quodlibet, along with the Aria's bass line as the fancied "meat." Not exactly laugh-out-loud stuff. In any event, Baensch's extended metaphor rests on a verbal setup that appears to have been accepted uncritically by countless scholars and enthusiasts.

So, in addition to the question of whether the character of the Quodlibet is truly jocular, there are related questions concerning the precise identifications of both of Bach's tunes as folk songs. Historians have searched high and low to confirm a link between Gähler's words and Bach's music.

The second tune proved less difficult to contend with. The structure of its melody is generated by the simple I–IV–V–I chord progression underlying a famous dance called the bergamasca. But a wide variety of texts were sung to a wide variety of bergamasca-inspired tunes. The music historian Paul Nettl reported in the 1920s that Bach's tune is nearly identical to one that shows up within a successive quodlibet published in Vienna in 1733 by Johann Valentin Rathgeber.[13] Here the words, however, are "Kraut und Ruben fressen meine Buben; hätten sie was bessers, wetzen sie das Messer" ("My lads wolf down cabbage and turnips; if they had something better, they would get their knife out").

It turns out that the text given by Gähler and Dehn was demonstrably well known in Germany in Bach's day. I have now found the whole thing quoted by Johann Lorenz Helbig in a 1701 book of sermons, where it is noted that "Cabbage and Turnips" was routinely sung by children, who "das Gemüss . . . weit nicht so

---

[13] Paul Nettl, "Die Bergamaska," *Zeitschrift für Musikwissenschaft* 5 (1922–1923): 294.

168 THEOLOGICAL CHARACTER OF SECULAR MUSIC

angenehm als das Fleisch [finden]" ("[find] vegetables not remotely as pleasant as meat").[14] Helbig gives the text as:

> Kraut und Rüben haben mich vertrieben;
> Hätt mein Mutter Fleisch gekocht,
> So wär ich länger blieben.

> Cabbage and turnips have driven me away;
> If my mother had cooked meat,
> Then I would have stayed longer.

What is more, I have discovered a nearly identical tune to Bach's, underlaid with words matching Helbig's, on a wrinkled sheet of paper depicted in the lower-left corner of the painting *Sitting Musician with a Pochette* (dance master's violin) of 1731 by Jan Philips van der Schlichten, a Dutch artist who was active in Germany (see figures 11.1 and 11.2).[15]

Regarding Bach's other tune, however, there have been intractable problems in finding any place where Gähler's or Dehn's text and Bach's tune appear together. For a start, in Gähler's version, "Ich BIN so LAN-ge NICHT bey DIR ge-WES-en," there are too many accented syllables to fit Bach's melody. Also, despite the massive holdings of folk-song archives in Germany, no one has ever been

---

[14] Sermon on Luke 2:33 in Johann Lorenz Helbig, *Weiss und Schwartz ... Feyertägliche Predigen* (Nuremburg, 1701), 296.

[15] This painting is listed, however, as "Johann Philipp von der Schlichten, 'Der Bettelmusikant' (1731)" in the Bayerische Staatsgemäldesammlungen, Alte Pinakothek, Munich. Its German title, which would be rendered *The Beggar Musician* in English, is not the artist's, and it is not at all clear that the musician depicted is indeed a beggar. Soon after the publication of my essay that the present chapter is based on (Michael Marissen, "The Serious Nature of the Quodlibet in Bach's Goldberg Variations," *CrossAccent: Journal of the Association of Lutheran Church Musicians* 29, no. 3 [2021]: 40–45), I was pleased and dismayed to see that this painting had been discovered independently by Edward C. Pepe, who reports in detail on his marvelous findings in "Zwei ikonographische Quellen für das Lied 'Kraut und Ruben' aus dem Quodlibet zu Bach's Goldberg-Variationen," *Bach-Jahrbuch* 107 (2021): 233–242. Along with the 1731 painting (not illustrated in his article), Pepe discusses a closely related drawing (illustrated at 240–241) by the same artist, thought to have been made around the same time.

Figure 11.1. Jan Philips van der Schlichten, *Sitting Musician with a Pochette*, 1731. Alte Pinakothek, Munich / Art Resource, NY.

able to find any version of Bach's first tune that properly fits any version of Gähler's or Dehn's words. I have now located at least a text-only source for their song that does properly mesh with Bach's tune. Within the spoken dialogue by Christian Felix Weisse that precedes the second musical number in Act III from Johann Adam Hiller's opera *Die Jubelhochzeit* (*The Golden Anniversary*) of 1773, a character is directed to sing just the words "Ich BIN so LANG nicht BEY dir ge-WEST, rück HER, rück HER, rück HER!" Nevertheless, it is worth noting that Gähler did not say that Kittel had claimed "Ich bin so lang" was Bach's association of text for his tune, and Gähler did not say anything about humor, either.

170 THEOLOGICAL CHARACTER OF SECULAR MUSIC

Figure 11.2. Jan Philips van der Schlichten, *Sitting Musician with a Pochette*, 1731, detail.
Alte Pinakothek, Munich / Art Resource, NY.

Kittel's identification is most likely a "zebra" (from the medical-diagnostics aphorism, "When you hear hoofbeats behind you, do not expect to see a zebra"). The more likely "horse" that people in Bach's milieu would instantly have envisaged was the exceptionally familiar Lutheran hymn tune "Was GOTT tut, DAS ist WOHL-ge-TAN" ("What God Does, That Is Done Well"), a melody as well known to them as "Happy Birthday" is to the general public today (see example 11.1).[16] With the hymn, Bach's Quodlibet could be

---

[16] Occasionally, a similarity to "Was Gott tut" is mentioned by writers on Bach, but the scholarly literature has not entertained this as the most likely association for Bach's Quodlibet, on account of the purportedly established "fact" that Bach's source was the folk song "Ich bin so lang nicht bey dir g'west." For a key example, see Christoph Wolff's

Example 11.1

heard as proclaiming that ultimately the *Goldberg Variations* were God's handiwork, not Bach's alone. Signing off in this way would certainly chime well with Bach's frequent practice of inscribing "Soli Deo gloria" ("To God alone the glory") at the end of his musical scores.[17]

How, then, might Bach's use of this hymn tune jibe with his use of the other tune, "Cabbage and Turnips"? In several

passing assessment in his *Kritischer Bericht for Johann Sebastian Bach, Neue Ausgabe sämtlicher Werke*, series V, vol. 2, *Vierter Teil der Klavierübung* (Kassel: Bärenreiter, 1981), 112: "Although the melody [that Bach quoted in part—the folk song 'Ich bin so lang'] is in its entirety no longer at hand, [it may at least be mentioned that] the same incipit is found in a range of further folk tunes or even sacred melodies ['oder auch geistliche Melodien'] (e.g., 'Was Gott tut, das ist wohlgetan')." If the melody is indeed "Was Gott tut," then its slight alteration to have it end on the *re* instead of the *mi* note of the scale here would be understood as accommodating the constraints of the Quodlibet's counterpoint. For a similar alteration, see the end of the head phrase in the opening chorus from Bach's church cantata *Himmelskönig, sei willkommen* (BWV 182), which is obviously a quotation of the hymn tune "Jesu, deine Passion" as it appears in bars 42–45 of the soprano line in movement 7 of this same cantata. (See also Bach's half-step alteration to the whole-step ending of the first *Kraut-*and*-Rüben* phrase at bar 6 in the *Goldbergs* Quodlibet.)

[17] For a close consideration of this practice of Bach's, see Marissen, "Bach against Modernity" (reprinted as chapter 1 in the present volume).

eighteenth-century German dictionaries, the word "quodlibet" was defined as "ein Durcheinander" ("a hodgepodge"). There were also various expressions in the vein of "Es liegt wie Kraut und Rüben durcheinander" ("It is like cabbage and turnips in a hodgepodge"). Just as van der Schlichten's painting is a visual "Kraut-und-Rüben," where musical and domestic objects are mindfully strewn about the room, Bach's Quodlibet is a sonic "Kraut-und-Rüben," where contrasting spiritual and worldly songs are harmoniously pitched together above a prior bass line.

While there is plenty of humorous material to seek in Bach,[18] it seems the *Goldbergs* Quodlibet is not a good place to find it. Some performers and listeners, and even Herr Bach himself, may well have smiled with pleasure at its extremely clever and witty combination of hymn and folk song, but in light of new evidence, the now traditional notion that the *Goldbergs* Quodlibet would have been received as simply jocular does look rather unlikely.

What is so remarkable and marvelous about the concordant motley "space" of Bach's joyous Quodlibet is that—as with such sublime quodlibets as "You're Just in Love" from Irving Berlin's *Call Me Madam*[19]—the whole is a lot more than the sum of its parts.

In many segments of the real world of eighteenth-century Europe, the authoritative voices of Enlightenment reason, individual experience, and art-as-entertainment were getting louder and louder. But throughout the world of Bach's music, most palpably and impressively in the Quodlibet from his *Goldberg Variations*, the suprapersonal spheres of the "secular" and the "sacred" were put forward together in an all-embracing harmony. Bach would have written the *Goldberg Variations* not as jokesome entertainment or as self-expression but as an act of premodern Lutheran tribute to the heavenly and earthly realms of God.

---

[18] See esp. David Yearsley, "Bach the Humorist," in *Rethinking Bach*, ed. Bettina Varwig (New York: Oxford University Press, 2021), 193–225.

[19] https://www.youtube.com/watch?v=2LAijDQ2cIE. My thanks to Eric Schorr for this reference.

Works Cited

Adelung, Johann Christoph. *Grammatisch-Kritisches Wörterbuch der Hochdeutschen Mundart (Ausgabe letzter Hand, Leipzig 1793–1801).* Digitized version in Wörterbuchnetz des Trier Center for Digital Humanities, Version 01/21. https://www.woerterbuchnetz.de/Adelung.

Ambrose, Z. Philip. *J. S. Bach: The Vocal Texts in English Translation with Commentary: Third Revised Edition.* Bloomington, IN: Xlibris, 2020.

Arnold, Denis. *Bach.* New York: Oxford University Press, 1984.

Bach, Johann Sebastian. *Erhalt uns, Herr, bei deinem Wort, BWV 126.* Edited by Karin Wollschläger. Stuttgarter Bach-Ausgaben: Urtext. Stuttgart: Carus-Verlag, 2012.

Baensch, Otto. "Nochmals das Quodlibet der Goldbergvariationen." *Zeitschrift für Musik* 101 (1934): 322–323.

Begbie, Jeremy. "Bach and Theology." In *Rethinking Bach*, edited by Bettina Varwig, 169–192. New York: Oxford University Press, 2021.

Begbie, Jeremy. "Disquieting Conversations: Bach, Modernity, and God." In *Music, Modernity, and God*, by Jeremy Begbie, 41–72. New York: Oxford University Press, 2013.

Belfer, Lauren. *And After the Fire.* New York: Harper, 2016.

Berger, Karol. *Bach's Cycle, Mozart's Arrow: An Essay on the Origins of Musical Modernity.* Berkeley: University of California Press, 2007.

Bitter, Carl Hermann. *Johann Sebastian Bach.* Berlin: Wilhelm Baensch, 1881.

Blanken, Christine, Christoph Wolff, and Peter Wollny. *Bach-Werke-Verzeichnis (BWV): Thematisch-systematisches Verzeichnis der musikalischen Werke von Johann Sebastian Bach.* 3rd ed. Wiesbaden: Breitkopf & Härtel, 2022.

Butt, John. *Bach Interpretation: Articulation Markings in the Primary Sources of J. S. Bach.* Cambridge: Cambridge University Press, 1990.

Butt, John. *Bach's Dialogue with Modernity: Perspectives on the Passions.* Cambridge: Cambridge University Press, 2010.

Butt, John. "Bach's Metaphysics of Music." In *The Cambridge Companion to Bach*, edited by John Butt, 46–59. Cambridge: Cambridge University Press, 1997.

Calov, Abraham. *Die heilige Bibel nach S. Herrn D. Martini Lutheri Deutscher Dolmetschung und Erklärung.* VI parts. Wittenberg, 1681–1682. Color facsimile: Franeker, Netherlands: Uitgeverij van Wijnen, 2017.

Chafe, Eric T. *Tonal Allegory in the Vocal Music of J. S. Bach.* Berkeley: University of California Press, 1991.

174 WORKS CITED

Cox, Howard H., ed. *The Calov Bible of J. S. Bach*. Ann Arbor, MI: UMI Research Press, 1985.

Cypess, Rebecca, and Nancy Sinkoff, eds. *Sara Levy's World: Gender, Judaism, and the Bach Tradition in Enlightenment Berlin*. Rochester, NY: University of Rochester Press, 2018.

Dellal, Pamela. "Bach Notes and Translations." www.emmanuelmusic.org/learn-engage/bach-notes-and-translations.

Drinker, Henry S. *Texts of the Choral Works of Johann Sebastian Bach in English Translation*. New York: Association of American Colleges, Arts Program, 1942–1943.

Dupré, Louis. *Passage to Modernity*. New Haven, CT: Yale University Press, 1993.

Dürr, Alfred. *The Cantatas of J. S. Bach: With Their Librettos in German-English Parallel Text*. Translated and revised by Richard D. P. Jones. Oxford: Oxford University Press, 2005.

Erickson, Raymond. "The Early Enlightenment, Jews, and Bach." *Musical Quarterly* 94 (2011): 518–547.

Erickson, Raymond. "The Early Enlightenment, Jews, and Bach: Further Considerations." *Understanding Bach* 9 (2014): 93–100.

Erikson, Erik H. *Young Man Luther: A Study in Psychoanalysis and History*. New York: W. W. Norton, 1958.

Fischer, William B. *When God Sang German: Etymological Essays about the Language of Bach's Sacred Music*. Independently published, 2017.

Forkel, Johann Nikolaus. *Über Johann Sebastian Bachs Leben, Kunst und Kunstwerke—Für patriotische Verehrer echter musikalischer Kunst*. Leipzig, 1802.

Gardiner, John Eliot. *Bach: Music in the Castle of Heaven*. New York: Knopf, 2013.

Gawthrop, Richard L. *Pietism and the Making of Eighteenth-Century Prussia*. Cambridge: Cambridge University Press, 1993.

Geier, Martin. *Zeit und Ewigkeit*. Leipzig, 1670.

Gerhard, Johann. "Vom Lob und Preis Gottes." In *Schola Pietatis*, by Johann Gerhard, III:398r–431r. Nuremberg, 1622–1623.

Grimm, Jacob, and Wilhelm Grimm. *Deutsches Wörterbuch von Jacob Grimm und Wilhelm Grimm*. Digitized version in Wörterbuchnetz des Trier Center for Digital Humanities, Version 01/21. https://www.woerterbuchnetz.de/DWB.

Grimm, Jacob, and Wilhelm Grimm. *Deutsches Wörterbuch von Jacob Grimm und Wilhelm Grimm / Neubearbeitung (A–F)*. Digitized version in Wörterbuchnetz des Trier Center for Digital Humanities, Version 01/21. https://www.woerterbuchnetz.de/DWB2.

Haselböck, Lucia. *Bach Textlexikon: Ein Wörterbuch der religiösen Sprachbilder im Vokalwerk von Johann Sebastian Bach*. Kassel: Bärenreiter, 2004.

Heber, Noelle M. *J. S. Bach's Material and Spiritual Treasures: A Theological Perspective*. Woodbridge, UK: Boydell, 2021.

WORKS CITED 175

Helbig, Johann Lorenz. *Weiss und Schwartz . . . Feyertägliche Predigen.* Nuremburg, 1701.

Herz, Gerhard. "Toward a New Image of Bach." In *Essays on J. S. Bach,* by Gerhard Herz, 149–184. Ann Arbor, MI: UMI Research Press, 1985.

Hoppe, Günter. "Köthener politische, ökonomische und höfische Verhältnisse als Schaffensbedingungen Bachs (Teil 1)." *Cöthener Bach-Hefte* 4 (1986): 13–62.

Kaussler, Ingrid, and Helmut Kaussler. *Die Goldberg-Variationen von J. S. Bach.* Stuttgart: Verlag Freies Geistesleben, 1985.

Kettle, Martin. "Bach at His Best: The Goldberg Variations Are the Pinnacle of Achievement on the Piano—András Schiff Gives Martin Kettle a Guided Tour." *Guardian,* October 3, 2003. https://www.theguardian.com/arts/frida yreview/story/0,12102,1054166,00.html.

Knoll, Mark W. "Leonard Reichle and J. S. Bach's Bible in Frankenmuth, Michigan." In *Er ist der Vater, wir sind die Bub'n: Essays in Honor of Christoph Wolff,* edited by Paul Corneilson and Peter Wollny, 207–224. Ann Arbor, MI: Steglein, 2010.

Kraft, Günther. "Zur Entstehungsgeschichte des 'Hochzeitsquodlibet' (BWV 524)." *Bach-Jahrbuch* 43 (1956): 140–154.

Leaver, Robin A. *Bachs theologische Bibliothek.* Neuhausen-Stuttgart: Hänssler-Verlag, 1985.

Leaver, Robin A. *J. S. Bach and Scripture.* St. Louis, MO: Concordia, 1985.

Ludwig, Christian. *Teutsch-Englisches Lexicon, worinnen nicht allein die Wörter samt den Nenn- Bey- und Sprich-Wörtern, sondern auch so wol die eigentliche als verblümte Redens-arten verzeichnet sind.* Leipzig, 1716.

Luther, Martin. *Aller Deutschen Bücher und Schrifften.* Altenburg, 1661–1664.

Luther, Martin. *Aller [Deutschen] Bücher und Schrifften.* Jena, 1555–1558.

Luther, Martin. *Colloquia oder Tischreden, so von Johann Aurifaber mit Fleiss zusammen getragen.* Halle, 1743.

Luther, Martin. *Luther's Works, Vol. 6, Lectures on Genesis: Chapters 31–37.* Edited by Jaroslav Pelikan, translated by Paul D. Pahl. St. Louis, MO: Concordia Publishing House, 1970.

Luther, Martin. "The Smalcald Articles of Christian Doctrine (1537)," translated by William Russell. In *The Book of Concord: The Confessions of the Evangelical Lutheran Church,* edited by Robert Kolb and Timothy J. Wengert, 295–328. Minneapolis: Fortress, 2000.

Luther, Martin. *Von den Juden und ihren Lügen—Neu bearbeitet und kommentiert von Matthias Morgenstern.* Berlin: Berlin University Press, 2016.

Marissen, Michael. "Bach against Modernity." In *Rethinking Bach,* edited by Bettina Varwig, 315–335. New York: Oxford University Press, 2021.

Marissen, Michael. *Bach & God.* New York: Oxford University Press, 2016.

Marissen, Michael. "Bach Was Far More Religious Than You Might Think." *New York Times,* Sunday Arts & Leisure section, April 1, 2018, AR10.

176 WORKS CITED

Marissen, Michael. "The Biographical Significance of Bach's Handwritten Entries in His Calov Bible." *Lutheran Quarterly* 34 (2020): 373–389.

Marissen, Michael. "The Character and Sources of the Anti-Judaism in Bach's Cantata 46." *Harvard Theological Review* 96 (2003): 63–99.

Marissen, Michael. "Historically Informed Rendering of the Librettos from Bach's Church Cantatas." In *Music and Theology: Essays in Honor of Robin A. Leaver on His Sixty-Fifth Birthday*, edited by Daniel Zager, 103–120. Lanham, MD: Scarecrow, 2007.

Marissen, Michael. *Lutheranism, Anti-Judaism, and Bach's* St. John Passion. New York: Oxford University Press, 1998.

Marissen, Michael. "The Serious Nature of the Quodlibet in Bach's Goldberg Variations." *CrossAccent: Journal of the Association of Lutheran Church Musicians* 29, no. 3 (2021): 40–45.

Marissen, Michael. *The Social and Religious Designs of J. S. Bach's Brandenburg Concertos*. Princeton, NJ: Princeton University Press, 1995.

Marissen, Michael, and Daniel R. Melamed. Texts and Historically-Informed Translations for the Music of Johann Sebastian Bach. http://bachcantatate xts.org.

Marschall, Rick. *Christian Encounters: Johann Sebastian Bach*. Nashville: Thomas Nelson, 2011.

Marshall, Robert L. "Young Man Bach: Toward a Twenty-First-Century Bach Biography." In *Bach and Mozart: Essays on the Enigma of Genius*, by Robert L. Marshall, 9–29, 261–266. Rochester, NY: University of Rochester Press, 2019.

Maul, Michael. *Bach: Eine Bildbiografie*. Leipzig: Lehmstedt, 2022.

Maul, Michael. "Der 200. Jahrestag des Augsburger Religionsfriedens (1755) und die Leipziger Bach-Pflege in der zweiten Hälfte des 18. Jh." *Bach-Jahrbuch* 86 (2000): 101–118.

Maul, Michael. "'Having to Perform and Direct the Music in the Capellmeister's Stead for Two Whole Years': Observations on How Bach Understood His Post during the 1740s." *Understanding Bach* 12 (2017): 37–58.

Melanchthon, Philip. "Apology of the Augsburg Confession," translated by Charles Arand. In *The Book of Concord: The Confessions of the Evangelical Lutheran Church*, edited by Robert Kolb and Timothy J. Wengert, 107–294. Minneapolis: Fortress, 2000.

Meyer, Ulrich. *Biblical Quotation and Allusion in the Cantata Libretti of Johann Sebastian Bach*. Lanham, MD: Scarecrow, 1997.

Nettl, Paul. "Die Bergamaska." *Zeitschrift für Musikwissenschaft* 5 (1922–1923): 291–295.

Neumann, Werner, and Hans-Joachim Schulze, eds. *Bach-Dokumente I*. Kassel: Bärenreiter, 1963.

Olearius, Johann. *Biblische Erklärung: Darinnen, nechst dem allgemeinen Haupt-Schlüssel der gantzen heiligen Schrifft*. 5 vols. Leipzig, 1678–1681.

WORKS CITED 177

Pepe, Edward C. "Zwei ikonographische Quellen für das Lied 'Kraut und Ruben' aus dem Quodlibet zu Bach's Goldberg-Variationen." *Bach-Jahrbuch* 107 (2021): 233–242.

Petzoldt, Martin. *Bach-Kommentar: Theologisch-musikwissenschaftliche Kommentierung der geistlichen Vokalwerke Johann Sebastian Bachs*, 4 vols. Kassel: Bärenreiter, 2004–2019.

Petzoldt, Martin. *Bachstätten: Ein Reiseführer zu Johann Sebastian Bach—Mit zahlreichen Abbildungen*. Frankfurt: Insel Verlag, 2000.

Petzoldt, Martin, and Joachim Petri. *Bach—Ehre sei dir Gott gesungen: Bilder und Texte zu Bachs Leben als Christ und seinem Wirken für die Kirche*. Berlin: Evangelische Verlagsanstalt Berlin, 1986.

Praetorius, Michael. *Syntagma Musicum III*. Edited and translated by Jeffery T. Kite-Powell. New York: Oxford University Press, 2004; orig. 1618–1619.

Rathey, Markus. *Johann Sebastian Bach's* Christmas Oratorio: *Music, Theology, Culture*. New York: Oxford University Press, 2016.

Reichardt, Johann Friedrich. *Über die Deutsche comische Oper*. Hamburg, 1774.

Rossin, Thomas Donald. "The Calov Bible of Johann Sebastian Bach: An Analysis of the Composer's Markings." PhD diss., University of Minnesota, 1992.

Russo, Richard. *Straight Man*. New York: Random House, 1997.

Schiff, András. *Music Comes out of Silence*. London: Weidenfeld & Nicolson, 2020.

Schulenberg, David. "'Musical Allegory' Reconsidered: Representation and Imagination in the Baroque." *Journal of Musicology* 13 (1995): 203–239.

Schulze, Hans-Joachim, ed. *Bach-Dokumente III*. Kassel: Bärenreiter, 1972.

Schulze, Hans-Joachim, ed. *Bach-Dokumente V*. Kassel: Bärenreiter, 2007.

Schulze, Hans-Joachim, ed. *Johann Sebastian Bach: Leben und Werk in Dokumenten*. Leipzig: Deutscher Taschenbuch Verlag, 1975.

Schulze, Hans-Joachim. "Notizen zu Bachs Quodlibets." In *Bach-Facetten: Essays—Studien—Miszellen*, by Hans-Joachim Schulze, 163–170. Leipzig: Evangelische Verlagsanstalt, 2017.

Schwartze, H. E. *Vollständige Jubelacten des . . . Religionsfriedens- und Freudenfestes der Evangelischen Kirche*. Leipzig, 1756.

Shabalina, Tatjana. "'Texte zur Music' in Sankt Petersburg: Neue Quellen zur Leipziger Musikgeschichte sowie zur Kompositions- und Aufführungstätigkeit Johann Sebastian Bachs." *Bach-Jahrbuch* 94 (2008): 33–98.

Shabalina, Tatjana. "'Texte zur Music' in Sankt Petersburg: Weitere Funde." *Bach-Jahrbuch* 95 (2009): 11–48.

Spitta, Philipp. *Johann Sebastian Bach*. 2 vols. Leipzig: Breitkopf & Härtel, 1873–1880.

Steiger, Renate. "Eine Predigt zum Locus De iustificatione: Die Kantate 'Jesu, der du meine Seele' BWV 78." In *Gnadengegenwart: Johann Sebastian Bach*

178 WORKS CITED

im Kontext lutherischer Orthodoxie und Frommigkeit, by Renate Steiger, 22–52. Stuttgart-Bad Cannstatt: Frommann-Holzboog, 2002.

Steiger, Renate. "'Gnadengegenwart': Johann Sebastian Bachs Pfingstkantate BWV 172 'Erschallet, ihr Lieder, erklinget, ihr Saiten!'" In *Die Quellen Johann Sebastian Bachs: Bachs Musik im Gottesdienst,* edited by Renate Steiger, 15–57. Heidelberg: Manutius Verlag, 1998.

Stock, Christian. *Homiletisches Real-Lexicon oder Reicher Vorrath zur geist- und weltlichen Beredtsamkeit.* Jena, 1734.

Stokes, Richard, trans. *Johann Sebastian Bach: The Complete Church and Secular Cantatas.* Ebrington, UK: Long Barn, 1999.

Talle, Andrew. *Beyond Bach: Music and Everyday Life in the Eighteenth Century.* Urbana-Champaign: University of Illinois Press, 2017.

Taruskin, Richard. "Facing Up, Finally, to Bach's Dark Vision." In *Text and Act: Essays on Music and Performance,* by Richard Taruskin, 307–315. New York: Oxford University Press, 1995.

Terry, Charles Sanford. *Joh. Seb. Bach: Cantata Texts, Sacred and Secular; with a Reconstruction of the Leipzig Liturgy of His Period.* London: Constable, 1926.

Trebilco, Paul. *Self-Designations and Group Identity in the New Testament.* Cambridge: Cambridge University Press, 2012.

Unger, Melvin P. *Handbook to Bach's Sacred Cantata Texts.* Lanham, MD: Scarecrow, 1996.

Varwig, Bettina. "Heartfelt Musicking: The Physiology of a Bach Cantata." *Representations* 143, no. 1 (2018): 36–62.

Varwig, Bettina. "Metaphors of Time and Modernity in Bach." *Journal of Musicology* 29 (2012): 154–190.

Wander, Karl Friedrich Wilhelm. *Deutsches Sprichwörter-Lexicon von Karl Friedrich Wilhelm Wander.* Digitized version in Wörterbuchnetz des Trier Center for Digital Humanities, Version 01/21. https://www.woerterbuchn etz.de/Wander.

White, Harry. "Evangelists of the Postmodern: Reconfigurations of Bach since 1985." *Understanding Bach* 12 (2017): 85–107.

White, Harry. "The Steward of Unmeaning Art: Bach and the Musical Subject." In *The Musical Discourse of Servitude: Authority, Autonomy, and the Work-Concept in Fux, Bach, and Handel,* by Harry White, 110–148. New York: Oxford University Press, 2020.

Wolff, Christoph. *Johann Sebastian Bach: The Learned Musician—Updated Edition.* New York: W. W. Norton, 2013.

Wolff, Christoph. *Kritischer Bericht for Johann Sebastian Bach, Neue Ausgabe sämtlicher Werke,* series V, vol. 2, *Vierter Teil der Klavierübung.* Kassel: Bärenreiter, 1981.

Wolff, Christoph, ed. *The New Bach Reader: A Life of Johann Sebastian Bach in Letters and Documents.* New York: W. W. Norton, 1998.

WORKS CITED 179

Wollny, Peter. *"Ein förmlicher Sebastian und Philipp Emanuel Bach-Kultus": Sara Levy und ihr musikalisches Wirken.* Wiesbaden: Breitkopf & Härtel, 2010.

Yearsley, David. "Bach the Humorist." In *Rethinking Bach,* edited by Bettina Varwig, 193–225. New York: Oxford University Press, 2021.

Index of Bach's Works

For the benefit of digital users, indexed terms that span two pages (e.g., 52–53) may, on occasion, appear on only one of those pages.

Ach Gott, vom Himmel sieh darein (BWV 2) 13

Ach wie flüchtig, ach wie nichtig (BWV 26) 16–18

Alles, was von Gott geboren (BWV 80.1) 97–98

Angenehmes Wiederau (BWV 30.1) 116

Ärgre dich, o Seele, nicht · (BWV 186) 13, 16

Art of Fugue (BWV 1080) 67

Auf, schmetternde Töne der muntern Trompeten (BWV 207.2) 131n.164

Brandenburg Concertos (BWV 1046–1051) 157–62

Brandenburg Concerto No. 1 (BWV 1046) 161–62

Brandenburg Concerto No. 2 (BWV 1047) 161

Brandenburg Concerto No. 3 (BWV 1048) 161–62

Brandenburg Concerto No. 4 (BWV 1049) 160

Brandenburg Concerto No. 5 (BWV 1050) 160–61

Brandenburg Concerto No. 6 (BWV 1051) 159–60

Christmas Oratorio (BWV 248) 40, 64–67

Concertos for Harpsichord (BWV 1052–1057) 158

Die Himmel erzählen die Ehre Gottes (BWV 76) 13, 16

Du wahrer Gott und Davids Sohn (BWV 23) 58–63

Ein feste Burg ist unser Gott (BWV 80.3) 95–98

Ein ungefärbt Gemüte (BWV 24) 25

Erhalt uns, Herr, bei deinem Wort (BWV 126) 20–23, 130n.159

Er rufet seinen Schafen mit Namen (BWV 175) 13

Erschallet, ihr Lieder (BWV 172) 77n.8

Es ist nichts Gesundes an meinem Leibe (BWV 25) 76–78

Falsche Welt, dir trau ich nicht (BWV 52) 161–62

Froher Tag, verlangte Stunden (BWV 1162) 131n.164

Geist und Seele wird verwirret (BWV 35) 13

Gleichwie der Regen und Schnee vom Himmel fällt (BWV 18) 20–21, 130n.159

Goldberg Variations (BWV 988) 163–72

Gott ist unsre Zuversicht (BWV 197) 13

Halt im Gedächtnis Jesum Christ (BWV 67) 161

182 INDEX OF BACH'S WORKS

He! kühne, m'e Tate!
(BWV deest) 142–43n.12
Herr, deine Augen sehen nach dem
Glauben (BWV 102) 68, 78–80
Herr Jesu Christ, wahr Mensch und
Gott (BWV 127) 164
Herz und Mund und Tat und Leben
(BWV 147) 92n.40
Himmelskönig, sei willkommen (BWV
182) 74–76, 81–85, 170–71n.16

Ich lasse dich nicht (BWV 1164) 62–63
Ich liebe den Höchsten von ganzem
Gemüte (BWV 174) 161–62
Ich will den Kreuzstab gerne tragen
(BWV 56) 92–95

Jesu, der du meine Seele (BWV
78) 89–92, 105–10

Komm, Jesu, komm (BWV 229) 139n.3

Lass, Fürstin, lass noch einen Strahl
(BWV 198) 101–5
Lasst uns sorgen, lasst uns wachen
(BWV 213) 13, 131n.164
Lobet den Herrn, alle seine
Heerscharen (BWV
1147) 29n.50

Mass in B minor (BWV 232.4) 30, 67
Mein Herze schwimmt im Blut
(BWV 199) 123

Nun komm, der Heiden Heiland
(BWV 62) 158
Nur jedem das Seine (BWV 163) 26

Orgel-Büchlein (BWV 599–624,
1169, 625–644) 8

Preise dein Glücke, gesegnetes Sachsen
(BWV 215) 28–29, 130n.158,
130n.161

Preise, Jerusalem, den Herrn (BWV
119) 161

Schmücke dich, o liebe Seele
(BWV 180) 13
Sehet, welch eine Liebe hat uns der
Vater erzeiget (BWV 64) 53
Sie werden euch in den Bann tun
(BWV 44) 141n.7
Singet dem Herrn ein neues Lied
(BWV 225) 41–42
St. *John Passion* (BWV 245) 64–65,
137–45
St. *Mark Passion* (BWV 247) 92n.41
St. *Matthew Passion* (BWV 244) 64–
65, 66, 138, 142–43n.12

Tönet, ihr Pauken! Erschallet,
Trompeten! (BWV 214) 128
Trio in C minor for Two Harpsichords
[anon. arrangement of *Sonata in C*
minor for Organ] (BWV 526) 151,
152
Trio in E-flat major for Flute, Violin,
and Continuo [composed, or
arranged, by Bach?] (BWV
1031) 151–52
Tritt auf die Glaubensbahn
(BWV 152) 13

Wachet auf, ruft uns die Stimme
(BWV 140) 85–88, 98–101
Was sind das für grosse Schlösser
(BWV 524) 164
Wer da gläubet und getauft wird
(BWV 37) 18
Wer Dank opfert, der preiset mich
(BWV 17) 112
Wer mich liebet, der wird mein Wort
halten (BWV 74) 160
Wer nur den lieben Gott lässt walten
(BWV 93) 160
Wo Gott der Herr nicht bei uns hält
(BWV 178) 12, 13

Index of Names and Subjects

For the benefit of digital users, indexed terms that span two pages (e.g., 52–53) may, on occasion, appear on only one of those pages.

Ambrose, Z. Philip 83, 84, 86–87, 91, 93, 96, 97, 100, 103, 109
Anti-Catholicism 20–23
Anti-Islam 20–24
Anti-Judaism 62, 80, 92n.41, 94–95, 114n.89, 137–45
Augustine 4n.2, 141n.8

Bach, Carl Philipp Emanuel 146–49, 151, 152
Bach, Elisabeth 64
Bach, Johann Ambrosius 64
Bach, Johann Christoph 64
Bach, Johann Christoph Friedrich 64
Bach, Wilhelm Friedemann 147–48, 151
Baensch, Otto 166–67
Belfer, Lauren 153n.7
Berlin, Irving 172
Bergamasca 167
Beweis 39–40
Bitter, Carl Hermann 142–43n.12
Butt, John 8–9, 14n.21, 19n.27, 142–43n.12

Calov, Abraham 6–7, 11–12, 14–15, 23, 24, 26–27, 28–29, 31–50, 88, 139n.2
Christian Ludwig, Margrave of Brandenburg/Schwedt 158
Chauvinism 25
Contempt, religious 19–24
Cox, Howard 41–42, 47
Cypess, Rebecca 150–53, 153n.7

Dehn, Siegfried Wilhelm 165, 168–69
Dellal, Pamela 83, 84, 87, 91, 93, 97, 100–1, 102, 103–4, 109
Drinker, Henry 75
Droysen, Gustav 148
Dupré, Louis 5

Fallacy, genetic 30n.52
Fallacy, reception 30n.52
Fichte, Johann Gottlieb 148
Forkel, Johann Nikolaus 151, 152–53, 166

Gähler, Casper Siegfried 164–65, 168–69
Gardiner, John Eliot 7, 36–39, 41–42
Geier, Martin 4
Gerhard, Johann 37–38
Gottsched, Johann Christoph 12, 13n.19, 24n.39, 104
Gottsched, Luise 12, 13n.19

Heber, Noelle 68–70
Helbig, Johann Lorenz 167–68
Hensel, Fanny 147
Herz, Gerhard 40–42
Herz, Henriette 148
Hiller, Johann Adam 168–69
Humboldt, Alexander von 148
Humboldt, Wilhelm von 148

Itzig, Daniel 147

184   INDEX OF NAMES AND SUBJECTS

J[esu]. J[uva]. 7–12
Jones, Richard D.P. 83, 84, 86, 87, 90–91, 93, 96, 97, 100, 102–3, 108–9

Kittel, Johann Christian 165, 168–71

Leibniz, Gottfried Wilhelm 12
Leopold of Anhalt-Köthen, Prince 29n.50, 157, 159
Levirate law 46–48
Levy, Samuel Salomon 147–48
Levy, Sara 147–50
Luther, Martin 11, 14–15, 23, 29, 43n.28, 46–47, 46n.32, 62–63, 77–78, 79–80, 91–92, 93–94, 110n.75, 112n.79, 126n.143, 139, 141–42

Marshall, Robert L. 45, 47–49
Meister zu helfen 107
Mendelssohn, Abraham 147
Mendelssohn, Felix 147
Mendelssohn, Moses 149
Mondegreen 33–34

Narcissism, cultural 30
Nettl, Paul 167
Neusner, Jacob 145

Olearius, Johann 88

Pepe, Edward C. 168n.15
Petzoldt, Martin 25–26n.41
Pietism 19n.27
Praetorius, Michael 164n.5
Progressive, Bach the 26–27, 32, 36–39

Quantz, Johann Joachim 151, 152
Quodlibet 163–72

Rathgeber, Johann Valentin 167
Reason, human 12–16, 29
Reichardt, Johann Friedrich 166
Rifkin, Joshua 42
Rossin, Thomas 41–42

Royalty 27–30
Russo, Richard 5–6

Salomon, Lea 147
Schiff, András 163–64
Schleiermacher, Friedrich 148
Schlichten, Jan Philips van der 168, 171–72
Schulze, Hans-Joachim 42
Sin, Original 14–15, 123n.129, 124n.132, 138, 141
S[oli]. D[eo]. G[loria]. 7–12, 170–71
Spener, Philipp Jacob 23
Spitta, Philipp 142–43n.12, 158
Stile affettuoso 160–61
Stile concitato 160, 161
Stokes, Richard 77, 78–79, 82, 84, 86, 87, 90, 93, 96, 97, 100, 103, 108
Stölzel, Gottfried Heinrich 144–45

Telemann, Georg Philipp 144n.15
Terry, Charles Sanford 74–75
Tolerance, religious 19–24
Typology 36–39, 43–45, 49–50, 79–80, 91–92, 99–100, 107, 115n.95, 127n.149

Unger, Melvin P. 82, 84, 86, 87, 90, 93, 95–96, 97–98, 100, 103, 108

Varnhagen, Rahel 148
Vocation 35–36
Vorspiel 40–45

Weisse, Christian Felix 168–69
Wissenschaft 17
Wolff, Christian 12
Wolff, Christoph 39–40, 50, 170–71n.16
World-Upside-Down 159–60

Yang, Yi-heng 152

Zelter, Carl Friedrich 149